The Canterbury Companion to the Book of Common Prayer Gospels

RAYMOND CHAPMAN

CANTERBURY
PRESS
Norwich

First published in 2013 by the Canterbury Press Norwich
Editorial office
3rd Floor, Invicta House,
108–114 Golden Lane,
London EC1Y 0TG

Canterbury Press is an imprint of Hymns Ancient &
Modern Ltd (a registered charity)
13A Hellesdon Park Road, Norwich,
Norfolk, NR6 5DR, UK

www.canterburypress.co.uk

British Library Cataloguing in Publication data

A catalogue record for this book is available
from the British Library

978 1-84825-568-5

Typeset by Manila Typesetting
Printed and bound in Great Britain by
CPI Group (UK) Ltd, Croydon

Contents

Structure and Purpose of this Companion

A passage from the Gospels is provided for every Sunday, and for many other occasions, in the service of Holy Communion in the Book of Common Prayer. They are mostly short and contain a specific episode, parable or piece of teaching. Together with the Collect and Epistle, they form the variable section of the service, leading from the opening words of prayer and exhortation to the sacramental liturgy, which is invariable except for certain Proper Prefaces. Hearing the familiar passage read aloud is a part of the total devotional experience, but it allows little time for reflection. Quiet consideration of the Gospel outside shared public worship enriches both personal devotional life and the grace of this great sacrament.

To this end, each of the Gospels in the Prayer Book is here presented in such a way as to focus on it in its own right as part of the precious record of the life and work of Jesus, with the constant awareness that it stands as an integral part of the worship which follows that work and offers its grace every day. The title of each Gospel is given as in the Prayer Book, with the precise reference of chapter and verses to enable the reader to augment it within its New Testament context if desired. The commentary that follows is intended to offer three aids to reading. First, the piece is briefly set in its biblical context. Then there is a reflection intended to draw out one or more ideas for application of what is read, concluding with an exhortation or challenge to apply the message personally. I venture to suggest these ideals of conduct and belief, only too aware that these contain aspirations which I seldom personally fulfil.

There follows a very short prayer, worded as an individual act of hope and supplication. Each section concludes with a passage from another source, intended to reinforce what has been offered, or to open a different approach. Some of these are drawn from direct commentaries on the passage for the day, others indirectly reflect some aspect of its meaning. As the Prayer Book Gospels have since 1662 been printed and read as in the Authorized or King James Version of the Bible, it seemed right to use this style of language for the short prayers, keeping them in line, and partly in structure, with that of the Collects. The usage of capital letters for the divine pronouns has been retained only where it appears in the quoted extracts. In the commentaries, the name of Jesus is regularly used, with only occasional variants such as Christ, Our Lord, the Saviour. Those who use these devotions are not likely to be unmindful of the divinity and saving grace of the central character, and as the Gospels are the record of the Son during his earthly incarnation, and the name Jesus is used throughout the Gospel records, this seemed to be the appropriate choice.

The Gospels in Personal Devotion

The Book of Common Prayer contains the liturgy of the Church of England, and was not designed as a book of private devotions. Nevertheless, its doctrine, language and spirituality have comforted and inspired people over the centuries. Many clergy, lacking regular company, say the required daily offices alone, and many lay people follow the same custom of daily prayer. Quiet devotion, help in time of need, guidance in perplexity, can all be found in prayerful reading. It may be helpful to suggest how the Gospel passages through the year can become part of regular prayer.

There is a Gospel for each Sunday in the year, to be used through the following week unless there is a major saint's day or other special commemoration. This book also includes the readings for weekdays in Holy Week, Easter Week and Whit Week, days which at the present time are not always marked by public services. Similarly, the saints' days, especially the lesser-known ones, may not be observed in all parish churches but still have much to offer the individual worshipper.

It is advisable to read the Gospel passage in the Prayer Book before and after reflection upon it. Begin with a simple prayer of commitment – 'Lord, open thou mine eyes, that I may behold wondrous things out of thy Law' – 'In thee is the well of life, and in thy light shall I see light' – 'Lord, bless and guide my reading' – or whatever occurs at the moment. Reading silently or aloud is a matter of personal choice; many find it useful to speak the words and receive them through the ear as well as the eye. Read slowly, prepared to pause and reflect at any moment: it is not a failure if the reading is not completed on any occasion. Sometimes a phrase will seize the mind, offering something relevant to the reader's situation and leading on to new insights and subjects for prayer.

It is hoped that the commentary after each reading will be helpful to direct the mind and devotion. These are not intended as definitive interpretations, or deep scholarly teaching, but suggestions to bring out something more in the words of which divine guidance has given record. Perhaps long and loving familiarity can sometimes make us less attentive, less receptive to new reflection; a new thought may come through new words. Even hearty disagreement with what is offered may be stimulating and productive! End with a short prayer, perhaps one of those offered here or with a simple 'Thank you' for the privilege of reading about the words and deeds of Jesus, and 'Please' for grace to follow him more nearly.

Above all, be relaxed, be trusting, be open to the guidance of the Holy Spirit. Think of what may lie behind the familiar narrative, the text which is beneath the text. For this is the word of the Lord, ever alive, ever new, to those who call upon him in faith.

Groups meeting for prayer and Bible study may find a similar method useful. One member of the group could read the passage aloud, followed by a period of silence and then discussion, picking up ideas from the commentary but all being spontaneous in expressing thoughts that come to each individual. Some groups may prefer silent reading by all before discussion, instead of one reading aloud. Again, there is no one ideal pattern for all, nor one that need be followed on every occasion.

Preaching the Gospel

Clergy and Readers know that there is no obligation to preach on the Gospel, or on any of the readings for the day. Nevertheless, there is much to be said for expounding the Gospel as part of the Ministry of the Word at Holy Communion. It may be five minutes at an early said service, or longer when the main service is eucharistic, but the Gospel is the focus of the first part of the service, leading to intercessions, confession, consecration and communion. The sermon follows the Creed, when we affirm the doctrines which are drawn from the Scriptures. (This is the only place in the regular services of the Book of Common Prayer where a sermon is required.) To preach on the Gospel has the great strength of expounding that which has just been heard, and which may be well known to most of the congregation but has been brought to fresh attention. These short commentaries are not intended to be sermon outlines, notes simply to be expanded to the required length. Spontaneity and personal reflection are essential in preaching. There may, however, be some points which arouse thought during preparation and fit into the preacher's personal message. It may be a piece of factual information, a reflection on the narrative or the parable, a thought from the suggestions of how we might respond to the teaching. If just one point is well developed as part of the sermon, much has been achieved.

A good sermon will combine instruction and teaching. Perhaps our congregations have few opportunities to learn more about the Bible and Christian doctrine after Confirmation classes, which are not so regular as they were in the past and as the Prayer Book enjoins. Lectures and discussion groups have developed well in many parishes, but some do not attend them, and those who do will gain from the educational principle that good learning benefits by repetition. These short pieces are not complete guides. The one who preaches regularly will do well to assemble a small library of scholarly but accessible commentaries.

For many years after the English Reformation, there were disputes in the Church about the relative importance of sermons versus sacraments. This is no longer an issue, and it was always contrary to the spirit of the Church of England. Her priests are ordained with authority 'to preach the Word of God, and to minister the holy Sacraments'. Both are great and equal privileges and duties. It is a wonderful thing to be permitted to expound a section of the Gospels in a service at the heart of which are the words spoken by Jesus at the Last Supper, ordaining and empowering for ever the eucharistic offering.

A final idea, not only for regular preachers: these commentaries may give some help in writing a short reflection or a thought for the week in a pew-sheet or parish letter.

The Gospel at the Eucharist

The reading of the Gospel has been an essential part of the eucharistic liturgy since the earliest years of the Church. There were readings from the Scriptures in the Jewish synagogue services, and it was a natural development for the new Christian writings, both apostolic letters and the Gospels accepted as canonical, to have a similar place in collective worship. The Gospel took the place of honour near the end of the Synaxis, the Ministry of the Word, before the affirmation of faith through the Creed and the beginning of the Anaphora, the prayer of consecration and the subsequent communion. This pattern has been followed in most of the later liturgies; it is in the order for Holy Communion in the Book of Common Prayer.

The particular honour paid to the liturgical Gospel was marked by a number of customs and ceremonies. These are still fully observed in some of our own churches. More often they may be reduced or modified. To understand the importance of the liturgical

Gospel, it is useful to consider all that may be done. The Gospel is read by one in holy orders, although Readers are generally given this privilege today. It is the particular charge of the Deacon, whether one in Deacon's orders or acting as Deacon of the Mass. In the Prayer Book service for the Ordering of Deacons, the new Deacon is given a New Testament and the Bishop says, 'Take thou authority to read the Gospel in the Church of God, and to preach the same, if thou be thereto licensed by the Bishop himself.'

The Gospel book is carried in by the Deacon in the opening procession. At the time of reading, the celebrant blesses the Deacon, who takes the book to a central point in the church, accompanied by acolytes with candles and the thurifer who censes the book. A hymn or psalm is sung after the Epistle: this is called the Gradual, as being sung from the *gradus* or step from the sanctuary. Members of the congregation, all standing, face the place of reading, turning where appropriate. The Deacon signs the book with a cross, and announces the biblical book, chapter and verse for the reading of the occasion. Some of those present may make the sign of the cross on the forehead, lips and breast, to signify that the words they hear will be taken into the mind, told to others, and kept to be pondered in the heart. At the end of the reading, the book is returned in procession to the altar. These full ceremonies will not be observed in all our churches, and may indeed seem elaborate or unnecessary to some worshippers. But recalling them may remind us of the special place of the Gospel reading in our worship, and its importance for each individual beyond the time of the service. Standing to hear the Gospel, which is universally observed, sets it apart from the regular custom of sitting for readings, whether at communion or in other services.

The Gospels in our Prayer Book are derived mainly from the medieval usage of the Sarum, or Salisbury rite, which had become the order most widely used in England before the Reformation, and influenced the whole book. The first Prayer Book of 1549 reduced the number of special observances. Proper readings were kept for Sundays and major festivals, and for a few weekdays at certain seasons. Many of the lesser-known saints were removed from the calendar. The traditional Gradual was not included; the people were to say, 'Glory be to thee, O Lord' when the Gospel was announced: this response was omitted in the second Book of 1552. The reader would be 'the priest or deacon', and the Creed would follow immediately. This remained the usage for this part of the service in the Elizabethan Book of 1559. As the full communion service became less frequent, the Sunday morning service was often Matins, Litany and Ante-Communion, the latter including the Gospel, which thus retained its place in regular worship and, in its yearly cycle, would be continually heard.

The Book of Common Prayer as now authorized emerged from discussion between Anglican and Puritan representatives at the Savoy Conference in 1661. The result was not a new book, but a revision with some additions. At the Gospel was added a rubric, 'The people all standing up', emphasizing the special reverence due to the Gospel reading. One of the few adoptions of changes requested by the Presbyterian members was that the Epistles and Gospels should be taken from the King James Version of 1611. Other biblical passages were retained from the 'Bishops' Bible' of 1568, as can be seen for example in the Ten Commandments, the Comfortable Words and the Offertory Sentences. The proposed revision of the Prayer Book put forward in 1928 was not approved by Parliament but tolerated by most of the bishops and became the basis for the later Series 1 services. It made no difference to the reading of the Gospel except to add the people's words 'Glory be to thee O Lord' when the passage was announced, and 'Praise be to thee, O Christ' at the end. This practice is now followed in most churches.

The order for the Prayer Book Gospels is different from that of the Revised Common Lectionary used in Common Worship. The latter has a three-year cycle of continuous (though not complete) readings from each of the Synoptic Gospels in turn, with some interpolations from the Fourth Gospel. The Prayer Book readings range across all four Gospels, observing the concurrent patterns of the ecclesiastical year. The Temporale follows the life of Jesus from preparation for his coming during Advent, to the Passion, resurrection and ascension, and the beginning of the visible Church at Pentecost. The Gospels in this cycle mostly reflect the biblical record which they commemorate – the preparation in Advent, the showings of Christ's mission and power in the Epiphany season and so forward. In the long season after Trinity Sunday there is less continuity, and each Gospel has an event, a parable, or a discourse to be studied in its own right. Each has its own significance; different choices each Sunday keep us alert and open to a further aspect of the faith. We also move among the four Evangelists, with their distinctive style and approaches as noted below. Concurrently, the major saints' days and also week-day commemorations such as Ash Wednesday and Ascension Day have their own appropriate Gospel in the sequence called the Sanctorale.

What is the Gospel?

What is this Gospel which is proclaimed with such honour at every Eucharist? It is the *evangel*, the Greek *euangelion*, the good news. Our word 'gospel' is from the Old English 'godespel', which carries the same meaning. It is indeed a good story, and it is God's story. Its first appearance in the New Testament is at the start of Mark's Gospel, generally accepted as the earliest of the four: 'The beginning of the gospel of Jesus Christ, the Son of God.' That is indeed the beginning of our Christian faith, the news that the eternal Son of God took our human nature and lived on this earth as Jesus who was born in Bethlehem, grew up in Nazareth and died in Jerusalem. In him the Old Testament prophecies of the coming of God's Messiah were fulfilled. The word *euangelion* is used in the Septuagint, the Greek translation of the Hebrew Scriptures, in Isaiah 61.1 rendered in the King James Version as 'The Lord hath anointed me to preach good tidings unto the meek.' These are the words with which Jesus began his sermon in the synagogue in Nazareth; the KJV has 'to preach the gospel to the poor' (Luke 4.18). He tells the people present, 'This day this scripture is fulfilled in your ears', and his following words so incense them that they seek to kill him. This man is the Christ, the Messiah, the Anointed One. The words of the prophets have been proved true, the words

8

have come to their fulfilment in the Word, begotten of his Father before all worlds. That is the truth which is proclaimed wherever and whenever the Gospel is read, in private study or as the highest point in the shared Ministry of the Word.

The Gospel tells the story of the life of Jesus, his words, his deeds, his friends and enemies, the society in which he moved. It is not a biography as we understand the word. It is not read for objective knowledge, for increase in learning some of the facts of history, for pleasure or edification gained by reading of a good man. The purpose of the Gospel is the transformation of individual lives, for a personal relationship with God which is never changing yet always growing, felt in the secret soul, yet to be shared with others. It is good news for the individual and for the world. Its message of salvation culminates in the sacrificial death of Jesus, his resurrection and ascension. It has been said that each Gospel is the Passion story with a long prologue. It tells of the beginning of a new era, a new world in which the old world still has its sins and its sorrows but there is new meaning. It is necessary to emphasize these truths, familiar as they may be to many believers, because the Gospel has the outward form of being a book like any other, yet is different from all others, even the other books of the Bible.

This is why the Gospel has from the earliest years of the Church had its special place in the celebration of the holy mysteries which Jesus instituted at the Last Supper and commanded his followers to continue. This is why it is set aside by special observances, simple or elaborate, in the course of the liturgy. It is always to be received with renewed love and attention, familiar from continual hearing, always a fresh source of strength, assurance and hope.

The Four Gospels

The Gospel therefore is the record of the good news of Jesus Christ. From the second century, the word has also been used for each of the four separate accounts attributed to different writers. (There were others claiming special knowledge, some perhaps with authentic sayings of Jesus, but generally defective in narrative or doctrine.) Eventually these four were accepted by the Church as 'canonical', as authentic and to be believed.

The first three Gospels are known as the Synoptic Gospels; *synoptic* means 'seen together' and they have much in common which makes it possible to compare them. But each has its distinctive qualities and its way of portraying Jesus and his teaching. It is generally accepted that Mark was the first Gospel to be written and that Matthew and Luke drew on it. There was probably a source of other sayings of Jesus which they both used, and each of them has material found only in its own record. Certainly oral accounts of the life of Jesus were being used as a basis for preaching before the first written versions were made.

Matthew was the Gospel most highly regarded in the early Church, and was then believed to be the earliest. It stands first in the New Testament and is the Gospel most often used in the readings for Holy Communion in the Book of Common Prayer. Tradition identifies the author with Matthew the tax collector who was called to be one of the disciples (Matthew 9.9), though it was more likely written by an unknown author in Syrian Antioch. The Gospel begins with an account of the Nativity. This is different from that in Luke; it gives emphasis to the role of Joseph and includes the story of the Magi. It follows the ministry of Jesus from his baptism to his Passion, the sections of narrative being set around five main collections of his teaching. Its special value is its extensive record of the teaching which Jesus gave, including the long discourse known as the Sermon on the Mount. Matthew makes a strong point of how Jesus fulfils the Jewish expectations and gives the new Law to replace the old. He seems to have been writing for both Jewish and Gentile Christians, assuring the former that Jesus is the Messiah and the latter that all nations are included in the kingdom. He makes provision for some of the problems which were already occurring in the new community, such as litigation between believers, and questions about divorce (18.15–18; 19.9). The Passion narrative is notable for the repentance and suicide of Judas, and the dream of Pilate's wife. The resurrection appearances are preceded by a great earthquake and an angel opening the tomb, to the terror of the guard set to watch it. The disciples are told to return to Galilee to meet their risen Lord. There is no account of the ascension, though it is implied in the final commission to the disciples to preach and baptize throughout the world, and the promise that their Lord will be always with them. Matthew has much to say of the cost and obligations of discipleship, and the universal blessings of the gospel.

Mark, is the shortest of the Gospels. An early tradition assigns it to John Mark, the companion of Paul. He is said to have been with Peter in Rome and to have set down his memories of Jesus. Certainly Mark, followed by the other synoptic writers, does not spare the faults of the Twelve, especially Peter. He may have been the young man who fled naked from Gethsemane (Mark 14.51–52), leaving a kind of personal signature in the narrative. Mark has no Nativity story, but begins with a proclamation of the gospel, the good news of Jesus Christ, and the preaching of John the Baptist. There is less of the direct teaching of Jesus than in Matthew. This Gospel moves quickly from one episode to another – 'immediately' is one of Mark's favourite words – but it is not loose and unstructured. Mark's accounts are often brief, but he sometimes gives details not found in the other Gospels: breaking through the roof to bring the paralysed man to Jesus (2.4); the cushion in the boat on which Jesus was asleep during the storm (4.38). It makes much of the growing conflict between Jesus and the authorities and his greater conflict with the powers of evil. Jesus is presented as a hidden Messiah, ordering those whom he heals to keep silent, and warning the disciples not to reveal his true identity (8.30). The account of the Passion is particularly stark and sombre and the resurrection appearances are not described in the earliest manuscripts, which end with the words that the women at the tomb said nothing to anyone because they were afraid. Mark seems to have been writing for Gentile readers, for he often explains Jewish customs. He occasionally gives the exact words that Jesus used in Aramaic (e.g. 5.41; 7.34), translating them into the Greek which was the international tongue of the time. In this Gospel we are drawn close to the humanity of Jesus before his divinity is revealed, and to the fallibility of his followers who are yet sustained in faith.

Luke was with Paul on some of his missionary journeys and wrote the Acts of the Apostles which tells the story of the beginning of the Christian Church. He is described as a physician (Colossians 4.14) and he is often precise about some of the diseases which are miraculously healed. He is clearly a man of some culture, acquainted with both Jewish and Gentile society, who writes elegant Greek and is a skilful narrator. At the beginning of his Gospel he declares his intention of writing 'an orderly account' of the life of Jesus (Luke 1.3). He knew Mark (Colossians 4.10; Philemon 24) and used much of his material. He gives the fullest account of the Nativity, including the devotional songs attributed to Zechariah, Mary and Simeon, and the only record of the ascension. He tells of Pilate sending Jesus to Herod, and the resurrection appearance on the road to Emmaus. He also adds an extended account of the journey of Jesus from Galilee to Jerusalem after the transfiguration. He relates some of the longest and best-known parables of Jesus, such as those which are popularly known as the Good Samaritan and the Prodigal Son. He gives us the fullest account of the life of Jesus, emphasizing his compassion for the afflicted and for the outcasts of society. He shows Jesus as particularly sympathetic towards women, with a tenderness shown also on Calvary in the promise to the penitent thief. Luke has much to say of the power of the Spirit in the ministry of Jesus, which leads towards the account of Pentecost in the Acts of the Apostles.

John raises even more questions than the Synoptic Gospels. His account stands apart from them in not following the same common sources, and in having a different chronology of the events in the life of Jesus. There are no Nativity stories, and the Gospel begins with a Prologue which declares Jesus to be the eternal Word of God from the beginning, made incarnate for human salvation. The writer refers to himself as 'the disciple whom Jesus loved' and claims to be a reliable eye-witness of the events he records. Traditionally he has been identified as John son of Zebedee, one of the twelve disciples, though the exact authorship of this Gospel is uncertain. Whoever wrote the Gospel, his method is different from that of the Synoptics. He includes no parables, but records at length the sayings of Jesus, particularly those supposed to have been given after the Last Supper before the Passion. He is a sophisticated writer, marking the narrative with specific 'signs' in some of the miracles and giving to Jesus significant utterances beginning with 'I am'. He makes much of the image of light, from the Prologue onwards, and of the necessity of faith in Jesus as Son of God, one with the Father. He says little of Galilee and sets most of his account in Jerusalem, but places the last of the resurrection appearances by the Sea of Galilee. John has sometimes been called the 'spiritual Gospel', but this should not make the reader neglect the importance of his relation of facts and the specific settings which he gives to many events.

The Prayer Book Gospels

Sundays

The First Sunday in Advent
Matthew 21.1–13

Advent, the beginning of the Church year, may catch us between the lethargy of deepening winter and the pressing demands of coming Christmas. The season indeed leads us towards the glorious Nativity, but we should not start our Christmas activities too soon, as is the growing custom in our society. This is the time to be freshly alert to the wholeness of our faith. As the Epistle for today reminds us, 'Now it is high time to awake out of sleep.' Advent has many themes to keep us wakeful. It reminds us of the Old Testament prophecies of the Messiah, it points us to his incarnation, and it looks towards his second coming in glory. Advent is associated with meditation on the last things: death, judgement, hell and heaven, solemn thoughts which are often neglected today, even in the churches. The Gospel for the day looks towards the end of the earthly life of Jesus, the entry into Jerusalem which we call Palm Sunday. It presents the great truths revealed in him. The majesty of God, the victory over evil, is seen in the triumph with which his arrival is greeted, the shouts of 'Hosanna' – 'Save now'. The humility of his taking our nature upon him is shown in his choice of a humble donkey, not the warhorse of an earthly conqueror. The welcoming crowd does not know of the suffering that lies ahead for the one they greet with such joy. They do not know that not many years in the future their city will be destroyed and its people scattered. They do not know that the man on a donkey is the divine Judge who will return at the end of the age. We too cannot discern the future, but we have assurance that we are redeemed and our lives are in the hand of God. Now are the days for serious reflection, extra prayer, the calling to mind of sin and resolve for amendment. The cleansing of the Temple which ends this reading warns us of how easily we can fail in reverence towards sacred things and places. As the Church begins a new year, let us embrace again the new life which is for ever open to God's people.

Blessed Lord, entering thy holy city in humble triumph, enter into my heart and give me grace to keep this time with joy for thy coming, sorrow for my sins, and hope for new life in thee when my life here shall end.

This Gospel has been chosen for today because Advent time brings before us two truths, not one. If we were only thinking of the first coming of the Divine Saviour into the world, or only of his coming to judgement, passages of Scripture describing either of those momentous events would have been obviously appropriate. But, to do justice to the solemn time on which we enter today, we want to keep the two truths clearly before the eye of the soul. And, therefore, here we have a history in which they meet; a repetition; as it were, of our Lord's first coming to his own, when his own received him not; an anticipation of his coming to judgement, 'when every eye shall see him, and they also which pierced him'. For his entry into Jerusalem on Palm Sunday was certainly an act of grace. It was a last opportunity of embracing the Gospel, of learning who and what he was, and what he had to teach, and what he, and he alone, could do for those who would listen to him to any real purpose.

H. P. Liddon (1829–1890) *Advent in St Paul's*

The Second Sunday in Advent
Luke 21.25–33

At this time of new beginning, we are called to consider the end of all things. The Gospel warns us of the second coming of Christ in judgement, which we affirm at every Eucharist when we say the Nicene Creed. The ultimate fulfilment of God's purpose for this world of his creation is one of the continuing themes of the Bible, culminating in the strange and powerful imagery of the book of Revelation. In all our pleasures, all our troubles, we are never to forget that the things of this world are transitory, to be fully encountered but never to draw our hope away from the greater life to come. Scientists tell us that eventually life on our planet will become extinct; we know that our own individual lives in the body will end, whether the years of our presence here are long or short. Often we would rather not think of these things, and in this season we may be particularly distracted by thoughts of Christmas. The saying that the end was near has puzzled many commentators, and may have been drawn into Christ's prophecy of the coming destruction of Jerusalem. The first Christians believed that they were living in the last days. We do not know the unfolding of the years, but we might well pick up some of the urgency to repent and turn to God which is declared by Paul and other New Testament writers. Each day is new and unique, with its opportunities and temptations, its blessings and its trials. As our prayers and meditation at this time draw us towards the unknown future, the value of the present moment becomes even greater. All that happens here and now can be seen as a sacrament, an outward and visible sign of God's purpose working in us and in the whole world. There is heavenly peace to be found in our frenetic society, torn as it is by anxiety and uncertainty. The message of the Gospel is sombre, but yet uplifting. When the end comes, we know that our redemption is near, the righting of all wrongs, the final seal on the atonement already made for us upon the cross. The central image is not of death but of resurrection, of trees in springtime leaf, promising new life.

*Almighty God, Lord of all things past, present and to come, give
me grace to order my life according to thy will, while I move in
hope towards the greater life that is to come when thou shalt call
me from this world.*

> Before the mountains were brought forth, before
>   Earth and the world were made, then God was God:
> And God will still be God when flames shall roar
>   Round earth and heaven dissolving at His nod:
> And this God is our God, even while His rod
>   Of righteous wrath falls on us smiting sore:
> And this God is our God for evermore,
>   Through life, through death, while clod returns to clod.
> For though He slay us we will trust in Him;
>   We will flock home to Him by divers ways:
> Yea, though He slay us we will vaunt His praise,
>   Serving and loving with the Cherubim,
> Watching and loving with the Seraphim,
>   Our very selves His praise through endless days.

Christina Rossetti (1830–1894) 'Before the mountains were
brought forth', *Poems*

The Third Sunday in Advent
Matthew 11.2–10

John the Baptist is an important figure in our Advent devotions,
although, after the account of his birth, he does not appear in the
record until Jesus is a grown man, beginning his own ministry. John
is a link between the Old Testament and the New, the last of the
prophets proclaiming the coming of the Messiah, and the first to recognize the full divinity of Jesus. This passage finds him in prison,
consigned there by Herod, the puppet ruler of Galilee under the
Romans. John is soon to suffer a martyr's death like many of God's
messengers in the past and in the future. In his solitude he begins to
have doubts – is this man really the Messiah, or is there still another
to come? Jesus responds not with words of doctrine but by evidence

which all can see. The healing and life-giving miracles prophesied of the Messiah are being fulfilled. Lives are being changed, a new power has come into the world. Then he has a challenge for the questioners, then and in time to come. Did they go to see John out of mere curiosity, or with genuine hope? Do we spend too much time trying to satisfy our intellectual questions about the Bible and its teaching, taking time away from prayer and meditation? Are we like the Athenians whom Paul encountered, who cared for nothing 'but either to tell, or to hear some new thing' (Acts 17.21)? We are to be ever open to God's new revelation, without succumbing to the passion for novelty which is so widespread today. The desire to be better informed about our faith so that it may grow is wholly good, but it is the means and not the end in our walk with God. Jesus quotes from the prophet Malachi, the last book of the Old Testament, to confirm John's role as his herald to the world. We too shall give thanks for wonderful gifts received, and embrace the future hope which Advent brings.

Blessed Lord, thou hast given me so many signs of thy healing power and the strength that comes from thee alone. Give me a grateful heart to be worthy of thy love, and a tongue to make it known to others.

The Holy Baptist was separated from the world. He was a Nazarite. He went out from the world, and placed himself over against it, and spoke to it from his vantage ground, and called it to repentance. Then went out all Jerusalem to him into the desert, and he confronted it face to face. But in his teaching he spoke of One who should come to them and speak to them in a far different way. He should not separate Himself from them. He should not display Himself as some higher being, but as their brother, as of their flesh and of their bones, as one among many brethren, as one of the multitude and amidst them; nay, He was among them already.

J. H. Newman (1801–1890) *Meditations and Devotions*

The Fourth Sunday in Advent
John 1.19–28

The Jewish people were still waiting for the coming of the Messiah, foretold by the prophets, who would establish the reign of God on earth. Living under Roman rule, they were eager for liberation. When a new prophet came out of the wilderness, they were full of questions: could this be the Messiah, or his immediate forerunner? John answered them with honesty and wisdom. He would not claim even the role of a prophet, only to be a voice, speaking the words set down by Isaiah. When his own authority to baptize is challenged, he simply proclaims the authority of his cousin after the flesh, whom he knows to be his heavenly Lord, before whom he, and all his questioners, are unworthy. He knew his calling, and the inexpressible majesty of the One who had come. Perhaps we are sometimes more inclined to enquire about people's credentials than to listen to their words. We ask: Who are you? What training did you receive? Show us your authority. The message of God does not come only from those who seem to have special authority to speak. Holy wisdom may be given to the plain and simple ones of this world, put into the mouths of little children, especially dear to their heavenly Father. John the Baptist was a wild-looking figure, not respectably dressed, but he had the inestimable privilege of recognizing and baptizing the Lamb of God. On behalf of all the human race, he declared his unworthiness even to bend and untie the shoes of the Master. The timescale of the Advent Gospels may seem strange: from the triumphal entry to the second coming, then to the Baptist near the end of his life, then back to his first preaching. Perhaps it reminds us that what we call past, present and future are all one in the purpose of God. Those who came to meet the Baptist did not know that the time of waiting was nearly over, and few of them ever recognized the great signs that were to come. For us, Christmas is very near, our little waiting is almost over. But he who shall come is already among us and abides for ever.

Almighty God, in whose sight all time is as one, and for whom a thousand years are as yesterday, make me patient in times of waiting, trusting when the future seems uncertain, and ever humbly conscious of thy presence in my life.

It was necessary to give John's testimonies to the light, and to show the order in which they took place, and also, in order to show how effective John's testimony proved, to set forth the help it afforded afterwards to those to whom he bore it. But before all these testimonies there was an earlier one when the Baptist leaped in the womb of Elizabeth at the greeting of Mary. That was a testimony to Christ and attested His divine conception and birth. And what more need I say? John is everywhere a witness and forerunner of Christ. He anticipates His birth and dies a little before the death of the Son of God, and thus witnesses not only for those at the time of the birth, but to those who were expecting the freedom which was to come for man through the death of Christ. Thus, in all his life, he is a little before Christ, and everywhere makes ready for the Lord a people prepared for Him.

Origen (c 185–c 284) *Commentary on John*

Christmas Day
John 1.1–14

We are surrounded by words and images of the Nativity. This, above all the festivals of the Christian year, arouses the enthusiasm of a secular society, and also becomes a major commercial opportunity. We may well shrink from the temporary jollity, the excessive spending soon regretted, the failure to embrace the true meaning of the season. Yet not all is lost. More people come to church services than at any other time in the year. It is not for us to judge how God may enter the hearts of those who come with imperfect understanding. The sacred words of Christmas hymns sung as part of a social occasion may not be forgotten. Now more than ever we are to pray for the world that Jesus came to save. Our Christmas cards, the crib in the church, the words of our Christmas hymns, our readings at Morning and Evening Prayer, all draw our thoughts towards that night in Bethlehem. But when the Gospel is read at Holy Communion, we seem to enter a different world, to be told about the very nature of God. Here are truths beyond our understanding, wonders expressed in images of light, a proclamation to guide us in the great mystery. The eternal purpose of God is fulfilled in a moment of historical time. The One who has revealed himself in many ways and led his faithful servants towards the truth, comes into the world that he has made. The whole meaning of his creation and his love for the fallen human race now appears in a human body, a man who will grow, eat with friends and enemies, heal and teach many; will come to betrayal, suffering and death. Some will joyfully receive him and find a new reality in the presence of God, some will reject him. Humanity is brought from darkness into the light which darkness cannot hold back, cannot contain, as it shines in the world. It is right to make this season a festival time, for joyful worship, family love, a renewed sense of fellowship with all. These good things are signs of God's infinite bounty, and we dishonour them if we do not accept them with gratitude. But the true meaning of this day is not in the tinsel, the feasting, not even in the beloved crib. It is in four words of one of our Christmas hymns: 'God and sinners reconciled'.

God of love, thou hast given us thy greatest gift in the coming of the eternal Son to take our nature and for a time to live in this world, that we might live in him for ever. Grant me this day a joyful heart, and grace to receive him into my deepest being.

Signs are taken for wonders. 'Master, we would fain see a sign', that is a miracle. And in this sense it is a sign to wonder at. Indeed, every word here is a wonder. An infant; the infant Word, the Word, without a word; the eternal Word not able to speak a word; a wonder sure. And swaddled; and that a wonder too. 'He that' (as in the thirty-eighth of Job He saith), 'taketh the vast body of the main sea, turns it to and fro, as a little child, and rolls it about with the swaddling bands of darkness.' He to come thus into clouts, Himself! But yet, all is well; all children are so. But 'in a manger', that is it, there is the wonder. Children lie not there; He doth. There lieth He, the Lord of glory without all glory. Instead of a palace, a poor stable; of a cradle of state, a beast's cratch; no pillow but a lock of hay; no hangings but dust and cobwebs; no attendants, but 'in the midst of animals', as the Fathers read the third of Habakkuk. For if the inn were full, the stable was not empty we may be sure. A sign this, nay three in one, able to amaze any.

Lancelot Andrewes (1555–1626) *Ninety-six Sermons*

St Stephen's Day
Matthew 23.34–39

Just as we have begun our time of rejoicing in the Nativity of our Lord, we are called to remember a cruel and unjust killing. A very short time into its life, the Church receives its first martyr. The Gospel tells how, towards the end of his ministry here on earth, Jesus spoke of the many who would suffer for his name, and of the servants of God who had been brutally killed in the past. His human life was nearly over; the words of teaching had been spoken, the final sacrifice was near. In his divine foreknowledge of all that was to come, he could sorrow not for his own suffering but for the sickness and sadness of the world, especially those so near to him, a people singularly favoured by God, taught by the prophets, guided on their way. The peace which he had come to bring was not of this world. There would be suffering as well as joy, untimely death as well as new life. In the Jerusalem of the time, the holy city at the centre of the Jewish religion, there was neglect and deliberate disobedience to God's commands. In a tender maternal image, of the love which even a hen may have for her chicks, he gives us a glimpse of God's pain when his children will not accept the love which he is pouring out upon them. It is both bold and distressing to think of Almighty God suffering, yet we must know in ourselves how often we have grieved that heart of love. Does it seem strange, even inappropriate, to make this commemoration on the second day of Christmas? For many people it is the end of celebrations which they began in Advent, a second public holiday, Boxing Day; and if the name of Stephen is heard at all, it brings thoughts of Good King Wenceslas. What can the Christian learn today? First, that our faith is not all 'comfort and joy' and does not guarantee our continual pleasure in this world. Second, not to neglect our intercessions for those known to us or unknown, who are in any kind of distress. Many today are suffering persecution and even death for their steadfast love of Christ. And, third, to remember that to be a martyr means to be a witness, and that whatever our portion in this life, we are all called to be witnesses to the faith which blessed Stephen held fast even to death.

Almighty God, give me strength to be true to the faith to which Stephen thy first martyr witnessed to the end. Make me truly grateful for that same faith which I have received, and mindful of those for whom the way of truth is also the way of suffering.

Foremost and nearest to His throne,
By perfect robes of triumph known,
And likest Him in look and tone,
   The holy Stephen kneels,
With steadfast gaze, as when the sky
Flew open to his fainting eye,
Which, like a fading lamp, flash'd high,
   Seeing what death conceals.

Well might you guess what vision bright
Was present to his raptur'd sight,
E'en as reflected streams of light
   Their solar source betray –
The glory which our God surrounds,
The Son of Man, th' atoning wounds –

He sees them all; and earth's dull bounds
    Are melting fast away.

He sees them all – no other view
Could stamp the Saviour's likeness true,
Or with His love so deep embrue
    Man's sullen heart and gross –
'Jesu, do Thou my soul receive:
Jesu, do Thou my foes forgive.'
He who would learn that prayer, must live
    Under the holy Cross.

John Keble (1792–1866) 'St Stephen's Day'

St John the Evangelist
John 21.19–25

The name John appears several times in the New Testament.
Scholars conjecture about the identity or difference between the
son of Zebedee, the Evangelist and writer of three Epistles, and the
writer of the book of Revelation. Today we are concerned only with
the Gospel attributed to John and often called the Fourth Gospel.
It differs in many ways from the other three, which have much
material in common, and is sometimes regarded as more spiritual
or mystical, though it contains a great deal of narrative information about the life of Jesus, especially his times in Jerusalem. It is
certainly a very beautiful work, with many sayings of Jesus which
are not recorded elsewhere, notably the long Farewell Discourse
of teaching and comfort on the night before his Passion. Whatever
name he bore in his lifetime, this author appears in his Gospel as
'the Disciple whom Jesus loved'. It is he who is closest to Jesus at
the Last Supper, and who asks him about the identity of the one
who will betray him. He stands with the mother of the Lord at
the foot of the cross, and is the first to accept the empty tomb as a
sign of the resurrection. He sees and believes: the idea of physical
evidence coupled with spiritual insight runs through this Gospel,

with its many images of light. He is the first to recognize the risen Jesus on the shore of the lake and say, 'It is the Lord.' When we commemorate him by a piece from his writing today, we take another leap forward in historical time from the Nativity. After his resurrection, Jesus greets some of the Twelve on the shore of Lake Galilee where the calling to follow him had been given. The Gospel which begins by telling the wonderful mystery of the incarnation, read on Christmas Day, ends with a commission to carry into the new Church all that has now been accomplished. Peter has just been challenged about his love of Jesus, made to affirm it three times, bringing a painful memory of his threefold denial in the house of the High Priest, and told to take care of the coming flock of believers. Never suppressed for long, and always the first to ask a question, he wants to know what is to be the duty of the Beloved Disciple who writes this story. The reply, for him and for us all, is to follow where Jesus leads and not be concerned about what others must do. The message is underlined by the deliberate exaggeration about how much more Jesus did and spoke on earth. The message is for us all. What we are given is enough for us. Each one has a personal calling and the record which we have is all we need to guide us.

Dear Lord, let me not seek to know what is beyond my understanding, or to be curious about what others are called to do in thy name, but, while I walk this earth, to follow in faith the way that is set before me, guided by the message of Holy Scripture.

Word supreme, before creation
Born of God eternally
Who didst will for our salvation
To be born on earth, and die;
Well thy saints have kept their station,
Watching till thine hour drew nigh.
Now 'tis come, and faith espies thee:
Like an eagle in the morn,
John in steadfast worship eyes thee,
Thy belov'd, thy latest born:

In thy glory he descries thee
Reigning from the tree of scorn.
He first hoping and believing
Did beside the grave adore;
Latest he, the warfare leaving,
Landed on the eternal shore;
And his witness we receiving
Own thee Lord for evermore.
Much he asked in loving wonder,
On thy bosom leaning, Lord!
In that secret place of thunder,
Answer kind didst thou accord,
Wisdom for thy Church to ponder
Till the day of dread award.

John Keble (1792–1866) 'St John's Day'

The Innocents' Day
Matthew 2.13–18

Because a child was born, a man became the first of a long line
of people who suffered death for their faith. Because a child was
born, another man was given insight into the deep mysteries of
that faith. Because a child was born, other children were wantonly
killed in an attempt to destroy what seemed to be a threat to tyr-
anny. The Magi had brought precious gifts, but they had left a
legacy of distress for the little town where they had worshipped,
and for the region around it. The world had changed, pardoned
and redeemed by the child in Bethlehem, yet in that same town a
massacre seemed to say that nothing had changed, that the acts
of cruelty and injustice, recorded in the Jewish Scriptures and in
many secular histories, would continue for ever. The suffering of
the innocent, particularly the suffering of children, is one of the
greatest problems in our faith – far more demanding than trying to
relate to the articles of the Creeds. It seems to question belief in a
loving God, a debate which is most deeply engaged in the book of

Job. We know too well that suffering is all around us, among those we know, and in distant parts of the world which seem beyond our aid. We try to reach out through intercessory prayer, and hope that our love somehow touches the pain of others whom we cannot know. This brief, agonizing, story points to the heart of the whole Christian gospel, which comes to a climax in a bitter and shameful death and ends with greater life restored. How far all this moves from the joyful worship of Christmas Day? The pure happiness of the Nativity is not destroyed, and our celebration will continue, but we are reminded that 'rejoice and be merry' is not the song of every human heart, now or at any time. Joy and sorrow are always mingled in Christian faith and observance. Whenever we celebrate Holy Communion, it is the Eucharist, the great thanksgiving, but at its heart is commemoration of the Last Supper and the sacrificial death which followed. Most of the saints who have special obser-vance in our calendar were martyred for their steadfast witness. As we relax in comfort, we may be in danger of shutting out the sor-rows of the world, as the holy family was shut out from peaceful repose in Bethlehem. We do not live in a painless world, but in one where ultimately the meaning is love and the end is salvation.

God our Father, thou hast created this world in love and we have marred it through ignorance and deliberate sin. Let not my heart be hardened to ignore our human suffering, but give me eyes to see the pain of others and the grace to give help and comfort.

Farewell dear babe, my heart's too much content,
Farewell sweet babe, the pleasure of mine eye,
Farewell fair flower, that for a space was lent,
Then ta'en away unto Eternity.
Blest babe, why should I once bewail thy fate,
Or sigh thy days so soon were terminate,
Since thou art settled in an everlasting state?
Is by His hand alone that guides nature and fate.

Anne Bradstreet (c 1612–1672) 'In Memory of my Dear Grandchild', *The Tenth Muse*

The Sunday after Christmas Day
Matthew 1.18–25

Luke tells the story of Mary, from the annunciation to the Nativity
and beyond. Matthew begins with Joseph, called by God in a dream
like his Old Testament namesake, the son of Jacob. Joseph perhaps
seems to be a background figure in the Nativity story. In pictures
of the stable, or among the figures set up in the crib, he stands
silently looking at Mary and the child, where the whole wonder of
the scene is focused. No spoken words of Joseph are recorded in
the Gospels. He responds to the call of God by taking action, but
we never hear his words as we hear the words of Mary. Tradition
has seen him as an older man, and he disappears from the story of
Jesus before the great events begin. The last we read of him is the
time when he and Mary were anxiously searching for the boy Jesus
who had stayed behind at the Temple in Jerusalem. But Joseph was
called to be the human guardian of the Son of God, to protect and
guide him through the years of boyhood and early manhood, until
the time of the great ministry had come. When we first read of him,
his happiness seems to be shattered by fear that his betrothed has
been unfaithful. His essential goodness is shown immediately. He
will have no public scandal, he will bear his grief alone. Then he
receives the same divine message that had been sent to Mary: this
child is the promised Messiah, and he is to be given the name Jesus
which means 'Saviour'. Ahead of him there lies a weary journey,
a desperate search for shelter for mother and child, the flight of a
refugee from wanton killing, then years of unremarkable life back
in his native town. He is the pattern of unselfish married life, of
protection for the vulnerable, of trust in innocence when evidence
seems to point to guilt. He embodies some of the virtues which are
needful in the faith that Mary's child will bring to the world. That
quiet man in the stable is no background figure. He is a man who
has things to teach us 2,000 years later. When we are too ready to
think the worst of other people, to become distrustful even of those
we should most deeply trust, we might reflect about Joseph's dream
and consider whether the depth of despair may be the beginning of
a new raising to God's service. Often perplexed, often disappointed

and fearing the worst, as we wonder what to do next, God shows the way and calms our fears by a new revelation of his purpose.

Loving God, who didst guide and empower blessed Joseph to be the guardian of Jesus and Mary, grant me strength and assurance to obey thy will for me when my faith is tested, and keep me always compassionate for those who need my help.

Here is the clearest of instances of the distinction between doctrine and devotion. Who, from his prerogatives and the testimony on which they come to us, had a greater claim to receive an early recognition, among the faithful than he? A Saint of Scripture, the foster-father of our Lord, he was an object of the universal and absolute faith of the Christian world from the first, yet the devotion to him is comparatively of late date. When once it began, men seemed surprised that it had not been thought of before; and now, they hold him next to the Blessed Virgin in their religious affection and veneration.

J. H. Newman (1801–1890) *Sermons Bearing on Subjects of the Day*

The Circumcision of Christ
Luke 2.15–21

While many people, sadly, think that Christmas is all over, we are reminded by the continuation of the Nativity story that we are still in the traditional 12 days of Christmas. Indeed, we may regard the 40 days from Christmas Day to the Feast of the Presentation as the Nativity season, parallel to the 40 days of Lent and of Easter. This Gospel relates the reaction of the shepherds after the heavenly host had left them. Shepherds at that time and in that land were not regarded with the affection that is general in our own literary tradition, or with the respect due to the shepherd as the image of God in the Jewish Scriptures. Jesus would continue that image by speaking of himself as the Good Shepherd, but generally shepherds were

29

low in the social order. By God's grace these few men were greatly favoured, the first to hear news of the holy birth, and the first to proclaim it. The routine duty of a cold night was transformed into wonder and joy. Their tongues were loosened, they were given confidence to tell of what they had seen and heard. By contrast Mary, the bearer of the Son of God remained silent while she thought upon a mystery too deep for human expression. She humbly and graciously accepted her calling, as she had from the moment of the annunciation. These are examples for all who have heard and rejoiced at the good news of the incarnation. There is a time for sharing our faith, making known what God has done for us, and there is a time for prayerful meditation as we open ourselves to the unending wonder. This Gospel ends briefly but significantly in telling how Mary and Joseph conformed to the Jewish Law. The Son of God, born as full and perfect man, must fulfil all that was required of the people among whom he came. As they obeyed the outward Law, they also obeyed the angelic message which each of them had received, that this child, the Saviour, was to be named Jesus. Even their great faith did not reveal to them the full mystery of the event. The Son of God was made obedient to the Law of God, and human obedience became a sharing with the divine. The invulnerable suffered pain, and suffering would draw God's people closer to him. The mystery of the incarnation blends with the beginning of the calendar year: the gulf between God and the people of his fallen world has been for ever closed. And that too is a reminder for us: life goes on, and we must respond to what our faith commands.

God of all wonder, as thou hast given me grace to know thy beloved Son as my Saviour, grant that I may speak boldly of the Gospel message, and also meditate upon it so that I may enter more fully into its glory, in thankfulness and with obedience to thy commands.

This name 'which is above every name' has all things in it, and brings all things with it. It speaks more in five letters than we can do in five thousand words. It speaks more in it than we can speak today: and yet we intend today to speak of nothing else, nothing but Jesus, nothing but Jesus. Before his birth the angel announced that this child, born of Mary, would be great: 'he shall be called Son of the Highest, and the Lord God shall give him the throne of his father David.' The angel thus intimates that this was a name of the highest majesty and glory.

Mark Frank (1613–1664) Sermon 17, *Sermons*

The Epiphany or the Manifestation of Christ to the Gentiles
Matthew 2.1–12

The wise men have almost taken over presentations of the Nativity and become one of the most popular images on Christmas cards and calendars. Their guiding star has become a symbol of the season, in splendid isolation among shopping-mall decorations, or on the top of domestic Christmas trees. They crowd into the stable among the shepherds. Matthew's account makes it clear that by the time of their arrival the holy family had found better accommodation: the star stood over a 'house'. There is no hint that the men were kings, no sign of camels, or of material wealth except in their gifts to the Christ, which have been in only token amounts. These additions were made quite early in the Christian tradition, and it is easy to understand the attraction of the vivid story. For the developing Church it was a message of hope and assurance; the infant Christ seen first by people in and around Bethlehem, then strangers from the wider world, Gentiles whom the Jews believed were excluded from God's special choosing. The Epiphany is a showing forth, a manifestation of something previously known only to a few. The guiding star is one of the many examples of light as a sign of God's presence and power. We can see it as standing between the first command of creation, 'Let there be light', and the undying light of the new Jerusalem in the book of Revelation. It is the moment in history when the new Covenant was revealed, bringing hope and salvation for all humanity. As we continue to celebrate the Nativity while beginning a new calendar year, it is time to open ourselves to the divine guiding, to be ready to discern the signs of his purpose for each of us, and to be ready to follow until the calling reaches its consummation. For many, the end of the Christmas festivities, when the dusty decorations are taken down and the dry needles are swept up where the Christmas tree stood, marks a reluctant return to the routine of work in a cold month with half the winter still to come. For the faithful, the Epiphany season is a time of continuing glory, when the light that shone around the shepherds in the fields near Bethlehem is shown in the wonderful life which began that night. Light shines in a cold season and the people of God sing his praises and worship him in the beauty of holiness.

Heavenly Father, grant that in thy light I may see light, and be led like the wise men to worship and kneel in adoration, knowing the presence of Christ to be always with me. Accept my gifts of devotion, for they have their being only by thy grace.

Grace, thou source of each perfection,
   Favour from the height thy ray;
Thou the star of all direction,
   Child of endless truth and day.

Thou that bidst my cares be calmer,
   Lectur'd what to seek and shun,
Come, and guide a western palmer
   To the Virgin and her Son.

Lo! I travel in the spirit,
   On my knees my course I steer
To the house of might and merit
   With humility and fear.

Poor at least as John or Peter
   I my vows alone prefer;

But the strains of love are sweeter
  Than the frankincense and myrrh.

Christopher Smart (1722–1771) 'Epiphany', *Hymns and Spiritual Songs*

The First Sunday after Epiphany
Luke 2.41–52

This is the only reliable glimpse of Jesus between the return from Egypt and the beginning of his ministry. There are some infancy narratives, mostly containing improbable and magical stories, which were not accepted by the Church. Luke gives us this single episode of a time when the baby of Bethlehem has grown into the boy of Nazareth. Anyone whose child has been missing even for a few minutes will relate to the distress of Mary and Joseph, their frantic searching, and their mixture of relief and annoyance when Jesus is found. Then silence falls again for about 30 years as he grows to manhood, knows the life of a human family, and learns the ways of the world into which he has come. He is obedient to his human parents. He wins the approval of those who know him and his family, while he also grows more completely into the will of his heavenly Father. The perfect union of his divinity and his humanity is shown in these few verses. As so often, the Gospel combines narrative and teaching. As a boy nearing the age of admission to be a full male member of the Jewish community, he stays in Jerusalem not to find amusement but to go to the Temple and engage with some of its scholars. In later years he returns there to teach in his turn, and a few days before his Passion denounces its commercial abuse, violently cleanses it, and prophesies its destruction. In that boyhood episode, his parents lose him for three days and at last receive him back in mutual love. The events of the end of his earthly life, loss, grief, and the resurrection on the third day, are prefigured in what could be read as a plain story of a childhood misadventure which ended happily. Without trying to find deep symbolism in every word, our reading of the Gospels has very often something to say to us beyond its surface record. We should take time to meditate prayerfully on even the most familiar Gospel stories, so that we may learn more and more about the mysteries of our faith, and find in them guidance for our own condition. This is indeed a passage of epiphany, of showing forth. It may move us to try and pray for parents who have lost children by death or by later alienation; for all who do not know what has happened to any of their loved ones. We come into the season which leads from the continuing joy of the Nativity to the austerity of Lent. It is a time for self-examination, for learning to find the presence of God in the little things of life as well as in the times of worship and illumination. It is a time to remember that the signs of the revelation of God made flesh in Jesus of Nazareth are still all around us.

Blessed Lord, who in the years of thine incarnation didst know the joy and sorrows of human life, the call of obedience, the years of growth and learning, be with me as I journey through this world, and guide me to walk in holy wisdom to its end.

Thy kingdom come! Yea, bid it come!
　But when Thy kingdom first began
On earth, Thy kingdom was a home,
　A child, a woman, and a man.

The child was in the midst thereof,
　O, blessed Jesus, holiest One!
The centre and the fount of love,
　Mary and Joseph's little Son.

Wherever on the earth shall be
　A child, a woman, and a man,
Imaging that sweet trinity
　Wherewith Thy kingdom first began,

Establish there Thy kingdom! Yea,
　And o'er that trinity of love

Send down, as in Thy appointed day,
The brooding spirit of Thy Dove.

Katharine Tynan (1861–1931) 'Adveniat Regnum Tuum'

The Second Sunday after Epiphany
John 2.1–11

The Epiphany theme continues in this story, which is described as a 'sign' and a source of belief for those who were beginning to follow Jesus. He has grown to manhood, and now it is his mother who no longer shields him, but turns to him for help. His response seems abrupt, even harsh; we may see it not as a rejection of her call on him but as part of the growing realization of what lay before him even to the obedience of death. His glory is not yet to be fully manifested, but the compassion that is always in him now moves him to an act of kindness. The young couple newly married will not be embarrassed; the guests will not remain thirsty. But this is not a piece of human material generosity; it is an act of the divine bounty, which gives more than we can imagine or deserve. The quantity is enormous; if we take the measure of the jars literally, 120 gallons or more. Even allowing for the exaggeration which sometimes appears in the Gospels, and indeed in most records of the past, it is more than the occasion could possibly need. Here again, as in the Gospel for last Sunday, narrative and teaching go together. Jesus never uses his divine authority for his own benefit, even to Gethsemane and Calvary, but for the healing or comfort of other people. He uses the simple, necessary things of this world to carry out the work for which he came into the world. On this occasion, ordinary water and plain stone jars are enough for his purpose. So, through all the ages, familiar bread and wine are made the signs and the strength of his coming among us at every Eucharist. Here too, as so often, his love and power are shown not to those in high places but to the poor and simple. The 'ruler of the feast', perhaps a distinguished guest appointed for the occasion, does not know the source of the wine, but the servants who have carried out their orders are in on the secret. They seem to have kept discreet silence, perhaps overawed by the miracle they have witnessed; perhaps keeping the proper reserve which we feel when we have a special sense of the great power and love of God. The wedding feast is on 'the third day' as in due time was the resurrection, when the hour of Jesus had indeed come. The best wine has been kept to the last. All God's love as revealed in the previous Scriptures reaches its full and wonderful consummation in the new Covenant.

Lord, thou art the giver of all good things, for the body as well as for the soul: make me truly thankful for thy bounty, ready to serve the needs of others, valuing the simple things of this world which are channels for thy love.

That wine, which was produced by God in a vineyard, and which was first consumed, was good. None of those who drank of it found fault with it; and the Lord partook of it also. But that wine was better which the Word made from water, on the moment, and simply for the use of those who had been called to the marriage. For although the Lord had the power to supply wine to those feasting, independently of any created substance, and to fill with food those who were hungry, He did not adopt this course, but, taking the loaves which the earth had produced, and giving thanks, and on the other occasion making water wine, He satisfied those who were reclining at table, and gave drink to those who had been invited to the marriage, showing that the God who made the earth, and commanded it to bring forth fruit, who established the waters, and brought forth the fountains, was He who in these last times bestowed upon mankind, by His Son, the blessing of food and the favour of drink: the Incomprehensible acting thus by means of the comprehensible, and the Invisible by the visible; since there are none beyond Him, but He exists in the bosom of the Father.

Irenaeus (c 140–c 202) *Against Heresies X*

The Third Sunday after Epiphany
Matthew 8.1–13

Jesus has finished the long discourse which is commonly called the Sermon on the Mount. He has spoken of the meaning of the new faith, and its ethical obligations, particularly in relation to the old Law. As the people follow him, some aroused and many perhaps merely curious, he turns from spiritual teaching to physical healing. The first miraculous cure is related in a few words. There is a direct approach by the afflicted man, a declaration of faith, and an immediate healing as they stand together. The man is a Jew, one of Jesus' own people after the flesh, and he is told to fulfil the demand of the Law by proving to a priest that he is now clean. Then there is a longer and more surprising story. A soldier, holding a responsible rank in the army of the Roman occupying force, has heard of this man who does wonderful things, and he has recognized the signs of a greater power than he has known, authority which he can see in terms of his own military duties. Despite his position under the majesty of Rome, he comes humbly, admitting his own unworthiness to receive so great a guest. Jesus, in the accepted humility of his incarnation, is willing to go with the Gentile suppliant, but he recognizes the power of this unexpected faith from a stranger, and the centurion's request is granted by a distance healing. Mercy and grace come to the Gentiles; what the Magi offered in their act of worship will spread into the whole world. The kingdom is opening to all who will believe, with no other demand of age, status or gender. May that faith never fade in us, and may the humility of the centurion be our defence against pride and indifference. We must receive Holy Communion in perfect trust, but thinking, 'Lord I am not worthy that thou shouldest come under my roof.' And if judgement might come upon the Jews who did not honour their covenant, their heirs in the new Covenant must never be complacent. Here are lessons in simple faith, trust in the healing power of God, readiness to ask for our needs directly and without formal preparation or flattering words. Here too we see the unconditional love of God, the beginning of the time when as Paul writes, 'There is neither Jew nor Gentile, there is neither bond nor free, there is neither male nor female, for ye are all one in Christ Jesus' (Galatians 3.28).

Lord, I am not worthy of thy grace and love. I come as a suppliant, offering my faith in thy words of promise, weak and uncertain though it may be, and praying always to receive thy healing power for my body, mind and spirit.

I am not sufficient, O Master and Lord, that thou shouldest enter in under the roof of my soul, but since thou in thy love willest to dwell in me, I take courage and approach. Thou commandest; I will open wide the doors, which thou alone didst create, that thou mayest enter with compassion as is thy nature; that thou mayest enter, and enlighten my darkened mind. I believe that thou wilt do this, for thou didst not flee away from the sinful woman, when with tears she came near to thee, neither rejectedst thou the publican who repented, neither didst thou cast away the thief who confessed thy Kingdom, neither didst thou leave the repentant persecutor to himself: but all those who had been brought to thee by repentance, thou didst set in the company of thy friends, O thou who alone art blessed, ever, world without end.

John Chrysostom (c 347–407) *Greek Hieraktikon*

The Fourth Sunday after Epiphany
Matthew 8.23–34

Two more manifestations of Jesus as Lord continue the Epiphany season. Now we read of his power to bring calm, to take away fear and bring order where there has been disturbance. One of the storms which can suddenly come upon the normally tranquil Sea of Galilee fills the disciples with terror. Jesus is untroubled; Mark's account of this episode tells of him being asleep on a cushion in the boat. The disciples are in despair, abrupt in speaking to their Master, then deeply impressed by his command over natural forces. Lack of the faith which had been shown by the Jewish leper and the Gentile soldier brings a sharp rebuke. Perhaps their anxiety was increased because Jesus was now going to Gentile territory on the other side of the water, not just accepting the faith of a foreigner but actually taking his divine power beyond Israel. His first encounter in an alien place is with human disorder, as frightening in its own way as the unruly forces of nature. There is much in the Bible about possession by evil powers, some of it probably attributable to what we should now see as serious mental illness, but the reality of evil as more than human weakness, and capable of affecting people, is something which we neglect at our peril. Whatever its origin, violence and disorder recognize the ultimate power of good and know their time has ended. They must not trouble human life any more, but find refuge in the animal world. The almost casual destruction of the pigs is surprising and perhaps difficult to accept. The meaning may be that the local people are too concerned about material loss to be thankful for release from the men who had caused so much distress. There is something very sad, and very salutary, in the way that the local people ask Jesus to go away. They want no more disturbance, even when it has brought relief. They do not wait to hear if he has anything more to teach them. Do we ever feel impatient at the demands of the faith which we hold? There are things in the Bible that puzzle us. It is necessary to read with intelligence and be prepared to admit difficulties, but there is also a danger of letting intellectual curiosity over details interfere with the great message. This whole reading tells us that Jesus heals the mind as well as the body, and that evil is banished by his word. Every Christian, however devout, needs to take time for quiet reflection, and be open to what God is saying as well as what we are trying to say. We can find inner peace, and understand the beauty of the words, 'There was a great calm.'

Almighty God, author of all rest and calm, dispel the storms which may disturb my faith, create in me the silence where thy word can be received, and hold me ever within the beauty of thy peace.

The billows swell, the winds are high,
Clouds overcast my wintry sky;
Out of the depths to Thee I call.
My fears are great, my strength is small.

O Lord, the pilot's part perform,
And guard and guide me through the storm.
Defend me from each threatening ill,
Control the waves, say, 'Peace, be still.'

Amidst the roaring of the sea
My soul still hangs her hope on Thee;
Thy constant love, thy faithful care,
Is all that saves me from despair.

William Cowper (1731–1800) 'Temptation', *Olney Hymns*

The Fifth Sunday after Epiphany
Matthew 13.24–30

Like most of the parables, this seems on the surface to be a simple story, familiar in its ideas not only to farmers and in rural communities, but to anyone who has cultivated even the smallest garden. Weeds will appear, whatever precautions we take. We are unlikely to believe that someone has come over the garden fence and deliberately planted them, but it is perhaps hard not to think that there is something bad at work in the ground. Later in this chapter Jesus explains to his disciples the significance of the parable. The enemy is the devil, the reapers are angels, and their work is done when the world comes to an end. As we have it for this Sunday, it is a simple but dynamic story of good and evil, patience and wisdom. The servants are loyal and willing, but over-zealous in their wish to be quickly rid of the weeds. The basic message is clear enough: this world is essentially good, created by the loving power of God, but evil things have entered and made it a place where health and sickness, joy and sorrow, are intertwined. There is no neat explanation for human suffering, but there is no doubt that much of it is the result of human action, at best uncaring, and at worst with deliberate hate and desire to destroy all that is good and beautiful, finding pleasure in the power to inflict misery. There is also a warning that we can be too hasty in our judgements, too eager to get into action when the best solution is faithful waiting. Rushing into a difficult situation without thought can be as bad as deliberate indifference. God's purpose will become complete at the final judgement. Meanwhile he has a call for each of us in this world, to be answered willingly and faithfully, but with the wisdom which he alone can give. The Epiphany message is moving from manifestations of Christ's glory on earth to thoughts of consummation and final reckoning. When he came to be born as one of us, to walk and talk in the ways of human life, he brought mercy and grace without limit. He also brought new obligations, a more exacting but nobler set of precepts for our life here. Weeds have a nasty way of appearing even without deliberate human malice, and choking the good plants which we are trying to cultivate. The message is that we live in a damaged world, where all that is good will ultimately be victorious. Meanwhile, there is work to be done with zeal, but with discretion.

Heavenly Father, thou hast given good seed for us to cherish and grow in the garden of this world: strengthen me to resist evil, to walk wisely, and so to live that I may come to the fruition of thy purpose for me.

This parable of our Blessed Lord will bear the very closest inspection, because it shows us exactly what happens in everyday life; whether it be in the brightness of the morning, in the splendour of the noonday, or in the gloaming of the evening, it is all the same, this parable is the experience of everyday life. It is the experience of anyone who tries to do good in any way whatever, whether it be educational, whether it be patriotic, whether it be philanthropic, or whether it be Christian – he is sure to meet with the very same circumstances that this parable gives almost immediately. He may do his very best: he may spend his time, his money, his energy, his very soul, but he is certain to meet with the enemy who sows the tares. Sooner or later there is sure to be the enemy that follows after, as darkness follows light; someone is sure to come up who will question his motives, disparage his actions, assail his character. Wherever you sow wheat, the enemy follows you with the tares.

A. H. Stanton (1839–1913) *Last Sermons in St Alban's, Holborn*

The Sixth Sunday after Epiphany
Matthew 24.23–31

The season begins to draw towards Lent, and the Epiphany Gospels become more severe in their tone. This section comes near the end of Matthew's Gospel, which has much to say about the final judgement. We are drawn back to the Advent mood, now in preparation not for rejoicing in a new birth, but for remembering the cost of the redemption which it brought. The second coming of Christ in glory, called the Parousia, is an essential part of Christian doctrine, affirmed in the Creeds which we use liturgically. The warning against false expectations and claims to special knowledge is as relevant now as it was when it was first given. Through the centuries, people have predicted the imminent end of the world, freely applying the signs in the book of Revelation, and often giving a specific date and time for the cataclysmic day. The signs that Jesus prophesied have provided rich imagery to artists and poets. The point is that, literal or not, they are unmistakable in their intensity. The recurring errors and calamities of this world do not indicate its immediate ending. It is the reaction of people in every period of history, especially as they grow older, to say that things are not as good as they were and that the world is in an increasingly dangerous condition. The trouble at this present time is that this natural tendency is reinforced by the continual impact of news from all parts of the globe, usually it seems selected for its gloom. We hear of all human woes, not just those near to us. There have also been people claiming new revelation, not always connected with the Parousia, offering a new interpretation of the faith delivered through the apostles, forming new and exclusive sects for those who will ultimately be saved. As daily life goes on, the message is clear and simple: be alert, be sensitive to what is happening in the world, but do not continually look for signs of the end. Do not live in fear, but do not expect a sudden end to all our troubles. Do not listen to the charlatans or the deluded who would frighten us into changing our challenging but sustaining faith. We live between two worlds, and the visible earthly one is our present concern and where our duty lies. Everything is transitory, but we must live as if it were permanent. The novelist William Thackeray offered a simple pattern for the Christian's way of life. He wrote of a gardener who 'handled the roses provisionally, until the end of the world'.

O Lord God, the beginning and the end, give me grace to serve thee in this world with diligence, to know that there will be an end for my life here and for all mortal things, and to look in joyful expectation of my Saviour when he comes in glory.

The Catholic Church through all vicissitudes has yet endured. Body after body naming the name of Christ have arisen and seemed to succeed better than the Church for a time, generally through some defect in her teaching or character: for it has been generally through the fault of the Church that they have arisen, and on the neglect of the Church's duty that they have spread. But these bodies have not exhibited lasting power. Any great catastrophe which, as it were, shatters the structure of human society down to its foundations, brings to naught multitudes of enterprises which seemed successful. But there is one society which has exhibited a marked capacity for lasting, which after whatever vicissitudes has shown that it has still the power of recovery and persistence. This is that Church which is rooted on the word of Christ, which has the succession from His Apostles, in which are administered His sacraments according to His appointment, which holds to His apostolic tradition, and appeals back to His sacred Scriptures.

Charles Gore (1852–1932) *The Mission of the Church*

Septuagesima
Matthew 20.1–16

We all know that the parables of Jesus are simple stories, set in the context of their time, but with deeper meanings which speak to every generation. If this parable were to be taken as an exercise in labour relations, it would be disastrous – strikes, protests, demands for new legislation would follow any suggestion of the same wage for the same tasks, irrespective of working hours. The Parables of the Kingdom, of which this is one, often show a reversal of normal human values and expectations when the full purposes of God are revealed. This story in itself is simple. Men stand in a public place, hoping to find a job for the day; just as in the rural 'hiring fairs' in the nineteenth century, and the more recent crowds of workers waiting at the docks. The 'penny' is the denarius, the customary daily wage. The truth which the parable gives for understanding and reflection is that God pours out his love and mercy without measure for those who will accept his call. Wonderfully, spiritual grace is not measured on an assessment of good and bad deeds, but on dependence and trust, a sincere desire to live our fallible lives according to the faith we have received. In the words of the first Postcommunion Prayer in the Prayer Book, we ask God to accept us, 'not weighing our merits, but pardoning our offences'. There is more to be learned; as so often, the parable makes its strong point at the end. Those who had worked all day were jealous and resentful of those who had done only one hour. Are we sometimes jealous of those who come into our church community after a recent turn to faith, and are welcomed with great joy and perhaps given honourable positions? There may be a dangerous tendency to become complacent and self-righteous about a long and deeply grounded life of faith and church attendance. All that matters is obedience to the call of God, whether it comes early or late in life. The employer's rebuke of the discontented workers means, 'Are you resentful because I am generous?' It would be a terrible thing to be critical of the goodness of God to any but ourselves. There are many surprises, present and to come, in God's kingdom.

Almighty God, whose love and mercy are given without measure to all who truly desire to serve thee, accept my response to thy call, and give me true love for my fellow-servants as we labour together for the coming of thy kingdom.

O may we ever bear in mind that we are not sent into this world to stand all the day idle, but to go forth to our work and to our labour until the evening! Until the evening, not in the evening only of life, but serving God from our youth, and not waiting till our years fail us. Until the evening, not in the daytime only, lest we begin to run well, but fall away before our course is ended. The end is the proof of the matter. When the sun shines, this earth pleases; but let us look towards that eventide and the end of the day, when the Lord of the vineyard will walk amid the trees of His garden, and say unto His steward, 'Call the labourers, and give them their hire, beginning from the last unto the first.' That evening will be the trial: when the heat, and fever, and noise of the noontide are over, and the light fades, and the prospect saddens, and the shades lengthen, and the busy world is still.

J. H. Newman (1801–1890) *Catholic Sermons*

Sexagesima
Luke 8.4–15

This is one of the best-known parables of our Lord, perhaps because it has his fullest recorded explanation of the details. This kind of exposition has been attractive to many commentators on other parables, often useful but sometimes going too far in allegory and obscuring the main point. But here we have the divine wisdom to make the message plain. It is another story drawn from the life of its time, describing what would be familiar to all in that predominately rural land. The sower uses the broadcast method of scattering seed as he walks. Modern techniques are different, but every farmer and every domestic gardener still understands the problems which can interfere between seedtime and harvest. Also, what is said about the failures is still too familiar. Many hear the word of God but do not listen to it, and go on their way unchanged. Some seem to experience an instant conversion but do not persevere, do not try to develop the life of prayer and worship, and fall away when the life of faith becomes too demanding. Brief enthusiasm is easy, but lasting and unspectacular obedience is a different matter. Some decide that other things in their lives are more important, and gradually give up. In the strength of God, some persevere and try to live in the Christian way. There is warning as well as encouragement in the parable. None of us should ever feel complacent about our faith, however long it has sustained us. Remember the parable of the tares, and the dangers of temptation. Remember also that the good works which we may do are the signs of thankfulness and sincerity, not things to be laid to our spiritual credit. They come from the good seed of God, not from our own unaided decision. There is encouragement in Matthew's account of this same parable, which tells how the seed on good ground brings forth 30, 60 or a hundredfold, and that is also true for the human response to God's calling. While we aim for the highest, we know that he understands our frailty, and that even our feeblest efforts are accepted in love.

Heavenly Father, who hast given the good seed of thy word for our salvation, we are often barren soil, not responding to thy love. Fill me with the strength which I cannot find in myself, that I may grow in faith and bring forth good fruit in thy name.

At last comes the good ground. The good and honest heart. The ground is well prepared and receives the seed. How do you prepare ground for the seed? Do you know? Well, you must go over the ground and get up all the couch-grass. I know a little about farming. Get it well raked up, and tear it out of the ground by the roots – the couch-grass that grows. And I tell you what you do with it: you put it together in heaps and burn it. If you don't, it will take root again. Now, if you want to keep Lent well, you clear the ground a bit from the couch. Tear up the undue cares of life, and the deceitfulness of riches, and the pride of life. And if the heart be trodden hard, plough it up. But, mind you, get out the couch-grass; bring it together, put it in heaps. And as you go along, and see the little bonfires smoking all over the fields, say to yourselves, 'That is what I must do if I want to spend Lent well: get the couch-grass together in heaps and burn it.' And then, and then, in an honest and good heart, you will love the Word of God, and the devil shall not take it out of your hearts as you go out of the church. And if the world calls you a fool for keeping Lent, it won't scorch your religion out of you, and the weeds within your own soul won't choke the Word within you.

A. H. Stanton (1839–1913) *Faithful Stewardship*

Quinquagesima
Luke 18.31–43

Jesus begins his last journey to Jerusalem. The great signs have been given, many have been healed, many have heard the word of salvation. Now the way lies towards humiliation, pain and death. He prepares his disciples for the sorrow that is to come, but it is beyond their understanding. They cannot, or will not, accept that their beloved Master must suffer and die before his work on earth is completed. But until then, his ministry of love continues. He has just told more parables, received little children and said how precious they are in the sight of God, and sadly dismissed the rich ruler who is constrained by material wealth. He warns his hearers of the spiritual danger which potentially exists in the love of money. Knowing the fate which lies ahead for him, he does not withdraw to be alone but immediately responds to another human cry. The blind man comes in simple faith, a contrast to the negative attitude of the disciples. He is told to stop making a disturbance, but he will not be silent. His persistence reflects the story which Jesus has just told of the importunate widow, whose continual pleas eventually arouse the indifferent judge to action.

Full of praise and joy, he joins those who are following Jesus. Was it to the gate of the city, on the road to Jerusalem, even to the hill of Calvary and abiding faith? We cannot tell, this man shows us that the response to love is love returned, with thankfulness and praise. Distress and comfort, defeat and triumph, are made known in these verses. The disciples reacted sadly and uncertainly to the words of foreboding. The final words, that Jesus would rise again, were beyond their comprehension. In due time they would learn, come to know the whole truth, and be strengthened by it to new life. Through their record, the mystery has been revealed to us, who follow in faith, sometimes with imperfect sight, but in confidence and joy. Lent lies before us, with its call to remember our Lord's suffering, while we look towards its glorious resolution. The Epistle for today gives us a pattern for attempting this Lent, with hope and prayer, to follow the way of love which is revealed in Jesus.

Blessed Lord, thou dost ever hear the cry of human need, and dost respond in love to any who come in simple faith. Increase my faith, open my eyes to see thy glory, and lead me on to follow thee where the road leads, to bodily death and everlasting life.

At length! At length Jesus stopped! We read often in the Gospel that He waits. He knew the man was in earnest. It was good, perhaps, for His disciples to see how earnest the man was. I am sure it is good for us, too. And so He passed on. And when He had gone a little way on, beyond – at length, at length – at last it happened! The Lord Jesus turned. Yes, whatever you feel, you cry to God. We may despair of ourselves. We have a good right to, I admit, when we look through other Lents, and say, 'Well, you know, I am quite tired of my own experiences in Lent'. Yes, we may despair of ourselves; but never despair of the Master! He came all the way out of the ivory palaces of Heaven to save me. If you batter the gates of Heaven they will open; the hinges are oiled – with grace.

A. H. Stanton (1839–1913) *Faithful Stewardship*

Ash Wednesday
Matthew 6.16–21

So we begin another Lent, and perhaps wonder if we shall do better than we have in past years. The general response, made also by many people who do not always follow the rules of the Church, is to 'give up something for Lent'. The practice of fasting 40 days before Easter was accepted by the fourth century. Shorter periods of fasting, individual and collective, were part of traditional Judaism and were adopted by the early Church. The words of Jesus to his disciples make it clear that he regarded fasting as a definite duty, a 'when', not an 'if'. Equally he warned of the danger which he often condemned in the very pious of the time, of making a show of religious practice, hoping to gain both merit and admiration. What we might now see as the rather negative aspect of Lent is not to be taken lightly. Serious fasting may not be possible for many of us, but some abstention, some eschewing of a permissible pleasure, is an act of the will which creates an act of faith. The danger still is of being a little too pious in our words and talking about what we have decided to offer during Lent. Our Lenten rule is a matter of secret confidence between each of us and God. The principle of reserve, of reticence in discussing sacred matters, is good. The Gospel for this day leads from fasting to the need to lift our minds and desires above material things, an admonition never more needed than at the present time. Anxiety, pride, selfishness, are the consequences of being held by the values of this world. Lent is a time to find where our true treasure lies. The most positive Lenten rule is for deeper and increased devotion, in public worship, personal prayer and meditation, and spiritual reading. Above all, space to be quiet and open to the presence of God, not anxiously completing the chosen duties of the day, until there is no time for ordered silence. Through self-denial and deeper devotion, we may receive those 'new and contrite hearts' for which we pray daily at this season. Contrition does not call for a miserable face or a show of religious obedience. Lent should be essentially a positive time, a time to get back into training and improve our spiritual health. There is much concern today about physical fitness, commendable but sometimes almost excessive. The soul also needs its exercises, followed in humility and love. The 40 days of Lent are connected in our tradition and devotions with the 40 days when Jesus was in the wilderness, suffering physical deprivation and the assaults of temptation. Out of the wilderness experience there came the beginning of his ministry. We all have our wilderness experiences, some brief and passing, some deep and continuing to afflict us in our life on earth. Lent is a special time to offer them with faith, following the example of our Lord, the Suffering Servant who overcame the power of evil.

God whose presence is perfect peace and whose desire for us is perfect love, come to me as I begin this season of Lent, guide me to follow faithfully the rule which I desire to keep, let me grow closer to the Saviour through whom I have received all spiritual gifts.

Welcome, dear feast of Lent: who loves not thee,
He loves not Temperance, or Authority,
　　　But is composed of passion.
The Scriptures bid us fast, the Church says, now:
Give to thy Mother, what thou wouldst allow
　　　To every Corporation.

The humble soul composed of love and fear
Begins at home, and lays the burden there,
　　　When doctrines disagree.
He says, in things which use hath justly got,
I am a scandal to the Church and not
　　　The Church is so to me.

True Christians should be glad of an occasion
To use their temperance, seeking no evasion,
　　　When good is seasonable;
Unless Authority, which should increase
The obligation in us, make it less
　　　And Power itself disable.

Who goeth in the way which Christ hath gone,
Is much more sure to meet with him, than one
    That travelleth by-ways:
Perhaps my God, though he be far before,
May turn, and take me by the hand, and more
    May strengthen my decays.

Yet Lord, instruct us to improve our fast
By starving sin and taking such repast
    As may our faults control:
That every man may revel at his door,
Not in his parlour; banqueting the poor,
    And among those his soul.

George Herbert (1593–1633) 'Lent', *Works*

The First Sunday in Lent
Matthew 4.1–14

As we begin our spiritual journey, we remember how our Lord prepared for his ministry and the way to his Passion by 40 days of solitude and fasting. He suffered temptation, the experience of every human being and the consequence of his own perfect humanity. 'Temptation' is a word which, like 'love', is too often used carelessly and without thought. People may say that they are tempted to buy something expensive, to have another cake, to respond angrily to an insult. Temptation is a serious reality but it is not itself a cause for distress if it is properly understood. There are three points of temptation: the presentation, when we know the possibility of doing a wrong thing or refraining from a good one; consideration, when we find that this is an attractive thought; yielding, when we surrender to what has been presented. An old hymn puts it succinctly – 'Yield not to temptation, for yielding is sin/Each victory will help you some other to win.' As our sinless Lord was tempted, it is clear that temptation itself is not sin. He was 'in all points tempted like as we are, yet without sin' (Hebrews 4.15). In his wilderness experience, and all through his incarnate life, he did not use his divine power for his own advantage. He suffered hunger, would not persuade people by spectacular signs, refused the ultimate temptation to earthly power, as at the end he accepted the full human condition in Gethsemane and on Calvary. He countered evil suggestions through the word of God, and to this day the Bible, Old Testament as well as New, is our great resource. Lent may bring temptation more than any other season; it is when we are making spiritual progress, perhaps beginning to feel dangerously secure in our own strength, that the power of evil most often attacks us. The only way is to stand firm from the first suggestion, as Jesus himself did. He was triumphant over sin, then and to the end. In his account of the wilderness days, Luke says that the devil 'departed from him for a season' – for a short period of time. The battle was won, the conflict was not over. So it is with us, but if we trust in God the victory is assured. Matthew's ending to this account is different: 'angels came and ministered unto him'. There is so much in the unseen world that we do not know, and are not in this earthly life meant to know. When we read of devils and angels, we understand that there are powers fighting against God, and others which are mighty in his service. We may live on a battlefield, where our part is not to take the great decisions but to keep close to our heavenly leader, and be obedient to his every command.

Gracious Lord, as thou didst suffer hunger and the assault of evil for the sake of fallen humanity, grant me thy strength to resist temptation, to refuse the wrong way and choose the right, now in this season and through all my life.

Our Lord's temptation in the wilderness began with an attempt on the part of the evil one to make Him break His fast improperly. It began, but it did not end there. It was but the first of three temptations, and the other two were more addressed to His mind, not His bodily wants. One was to throw Himself down from the pinnacle, the other the offer of all the kingdoms of the world. They were more subtle temptations. Now, I have used the word 'subtle' already, and it needs some explanation. By a subtle temptation or a subtle sin, I mean one which it is very difficult to find out. Everyone knows what it is to break the ten commandments, the first, the second, the third, and so on. When a thing is directly commanded and the devil tempts us directly to break it, this is not a subtle temptation but a broad and gross temptation. But there are a great many things wrong which are not so obviously wrong. They are wrong as leading to what is wrong or the consequence of what is wrong, or they are wrong because they are the very same thing as what is forbidden, but dressed up and looking differently. The human mind is very deceitful; when a thing is forbidden, a man does not like directly to do it, but he goes to work if he can to get at the forbidden end in some way.

J. H. Newman (1801–1890) *Parochial and Plain Sermons*

The Second Sunday in Lent
Matthew 15.21–28

This story has one of the 'hard sayings' of Jesus, which are sometimes disquieting to faithful readers of the Gospels. His first response to the woman seems insulting, even cruel. Dogs are not greatly loved pets in the world of the New Testament. They may be useful as guards, helpers of shepherds, but they are not part of the domestic circle with attentive regular feeding. They are scavengers, lucky if they can creep close to a table from which scraps may fall. With this and similar episodes, we do not know the full circumstance: the spatial context, what had gone before, the tone of what was said. If the Evangelists thought fit to include these difficult bits in their record, we may assume that they do not detract from our Lord's ministry of love and compassion. It is important to read each story to the end, and meditate on the total result, not on the details. Here the first words may be taken as the predictable reaction from a Jew of that time to a request from a Gentile for a special favour. The woman is not deterred but recognizes

Jesus as Lord, Son of David, a man of power, worthy of great respect. Her reply is gentle and insightful, offering her lowly status to the divine compassion. Still today, many people are drawn to Jesus by what they have heard about him, and begin to seek him for help in their need. Sometimes their growing faith needs to be further tested as they are made to question their motives and the reality of their seeking. The words are harsh, perhaps the tone is questioning rather than dismissive, the face is kinder. The action is positive and restores health to the afflicted child. Now again a Gentile, on Gentile territory, is made equal in the love of God's Messiah, King of the Jews, soon to be revealed as the Lord of all creation, the conqueror of death. As with the centurion's servant, faith breaks down all human barriers and is recognized by another distance healing. It is a story which leaves us with no doubts, no anxiety, no feeling of bitterness or disappointment for the mother. Let us not overlook the response of the disciples, typical of their attitude to those who come to their Master for help. 'Send her away,' comes easily to them. Are they trying to protect Jesus from continual demands, are they jealous for their own privileged status, do they just not want to be bothered? As a bit of Lenten self-examination, we may well consider whether we have been discouraging to seekers after faith, or have restricted entry to our own little religious circle.

God of healing and love, keep me trustful and persevering in prayer, never discouraged by a time of waiting; and may I never fail to welcome and assist any who seek thee, never become selfish in the faith which I have been given by grace.

There is nothing which God loves so much as to be pressed by our perseverance and humiliation. It is this which increases repentance and faith; and it is this which our Blessed Lord means, when He says, 'the violent take the Kingdom by force', when the lukewarm give over at any delay or discouragement, the humble and earnest, on the contrary increase their humility and earnestness. They know that our Lord has Himself exhorted us not to be faint or weary in our prayers; to imitate the importunate widow, who overcame the unjust judge by her persevering entreaties; and the man at midnight calling long, in vain, to his friend, and never giving over till he had gained what he had needed. There is something of exceeding value and importance to our souls in long and unceasing prayer; and for this reason, Christ so often, in the Gospels, puts off and lingers long before He answered those petitioners with whom He was most pleased.

Isaac Williams (1802–1865) *Sermons* 1855

The Third Sunday in Lent
Luke 11.14–28

This is a Gospel passage rich in thoughts which are particularly appropriate in Lent. It unequivocally puts before us the problem of the evil in the world, whether we think of devils, or 'the devil', or have no certain idea of its nature. There is no getting away from the existence of something worse than human weakness, a force which is at odds with the beauty and benevolence of God's creation. Jesus faced the conflict all through his earthly life, from the temptation in the wilderness to the agony in Gethsemane and the final torment of the cross. His power against evil was so great and so spectacular that some of those who witnessed this act of healing thought that he was using some great demonic power to conquer a lesser one. This is one of the 'conflict' stories which become more frequent in the Gospels as Jesus arouses opposition until it leads to his death. He makes it clear that he is using no dark power, no kind of witchcraft or magic, but the power of God within himself. It is a terrible thing when people invoke evil things for earthly benefit; it is dangerous to seek for spiritual help in the unknown and outside the power of God as he has revealed it to us. There are today, as there have always been, cults which claim secret knowledge and power. Only God can bring the triumph of good over evil. The devil may be a powerful antagonist, but God is always greater, and his work reveals his glory. Jesus tells the sceptical crowd, and his words remain true for all times and all places, that they must decide where they stand. If we do not actively choose to live by all that is good, we are opposing it and holding back the work of the kingdom. Then comes the warning against self-satisfaction which is especially important while we try to make spiritual progress during Lent. It is when we feel most confident in our strength that we are weakest, when we are growing in faith and practice that we are most at risk. Immediate and sincere repentance of what seems a minor lapse, an angry word, a moment of envy, can make us feel more secure, more alert to the far worse temptations which are never far away. The hosts of Midian, as the well-known Lenten hymn calls them, do indeed 'prowl and prowl around'. We are certainly not to live in continual anxiety and self-questioning. But to get into the habit of shrugging off our frequent lapses starts on a dangerous path. The German theologian Friedrich Schleiermacher wrote that the sins of Christians, being continually repented, are continually forgiven. The mercy of God for repented sin is boundless, his holiness fills those who joyfully receive his word, those who do his will through firm faith and good works.

Almighty God, by whose power alone we can resist the evil of this world, shield me from false confidence in my own strength, keep me watchful against temptation, and confirm my faith in thy living Word.

There occurs in St Luke's Gospel a warning of the relapsed penitent. It is one of such fearful interest that perhaps nothing can be found to equal it in the whole of the Scriptures, so does it, in a few simple words, lift up the veil from the unseen world around us, showing us what our condition is, and telling us why we are so liable to a relapse, to fall again into a sin once admitted, and why, if this happens, it is so difficult to recover. Our Lord had first called attention to this point, that if Satan be driven out, this can only be by the power of God; therefore, to attribute it to any thing else is without excuse. But now, what awful consequences follow from this, for, if God alone can drive out an evil spirit, it is nothing but the protection of God which will keep him out, and if that protection is withdrawn, he will assuredly return. We know what watchfulness is necessary in everyone that has repented of past sin, and how liable he is to fall into it again without constant care; our Lord has, in a very fearful manner, explained to us how this is.

Isaac Williams (1802–1865) *Sermons* 1855

The Fourth Sunday in Lent
John 6.1–14

The story of the feeding of a great crowd is the only one of the miracles of Jesus which appears in all four Gospels, with some differences of detail but essentially the same narrative. To be thus preserved suggests that the first Christians regarded it as particularly important and needing to be remembered. It is a foreshadowing of the Holy Communion, notably in this Gospel, which does not relate the eucharistic actions and commandment at the Last Supper. Here in the wilderness, Jesus performs the fourfold action which is repeated by the priest at every Eucharist. He takes bread, gives thanks over it, breaks it and distributes it to the people. In John's account, the feeding is followed by a long discourse and dispute about Jesus as the Bread from Heaven. The whole narrative is full of meaning. A very small offering of simple things is accepted and used for the good of the people and the glory of God. There is not only sufficient for the immediate need, but more than can be eaten: what seemed totally inadequate is more than enough. It reminds us of the miracle at Cana, where wine in abundance was given when human planning failed. So too at every Eucharist a small quantity of bread and wine grows, not in physical size but in spiritual power, to feed the souls of all who will come. On a human level, it is good for us to note the reaction of the disciples to the apparent crisis. As usual, they are pessimistic and helpless, but they respond to what their Master commands. Philip and Andrew are singled out, two of the first disciples to be called in the Fourth Gospel, still not fully mature in their faith but willing and able to be used: a comfort and a challenge to all Christians who know their inadequacy and weakness. This Sunday is commonly called 'Mothering Sunday', perhaps from a former custom of visiting one's mother, or the cathedral, mother-church of the diocese, or the words in the Epistle about Jerusalem, 'the mother of us all'. It is also known as 'Refreshment Sunday' when some temporary lightening of the Lenten rule was allowed. It is a good time, halfway through Lent, to take stock honestly but not guiltily, in preparation for the coming demands of Passiontide. We may well meditate on the sacrament of Holy Communion here prefigured, the obedience and privilege of Christians from the beginning of the Church. Are we regular in attendance, honest in preparation, devoted in receiving, in love and charity towards those with whom we come to the Table of the Lord? In a great cathedral, in a little church, in a hospital ward, the love of God is given in simple things, and every celebration is true refreshment for the soul.

O Lord who dost feed thy people in body and soul, accept my thankfulness for thy generous love, and grant that I may always receive with reverence the precious sacrament of thy Body and Blood.

I saw the throng, so deeply separate,
   Fed at one only board –
The devout people, moved, intent, elate,
   And the devoted Lord.

Oh struck apart! Not side from human side,
   But souls from human soul,
As each asunder absorbed the multiplied,
   The ever unparted whole.

I saw the people as a field of flowers,
   Each grown at such a price
The sum of unimaginable powers
   Did no more than suffice.

A thousand single central daisies they,
   A thousand of the one:

For each, the entire monopoly of day
For each, the whole of the devoted sun.

Alice Meynell (1847–1922) 'A General Communion', *Oxford Book of Christian Verse*

The Fifth Sunday in Lent
John 8.46–57

We enter Passiontide, the last two weeks of Lent, when we resolve to strengthen our Lenten rule and increase our devotions as the Church moves towards the climax of Good Friday. The Gospel shakes any complacency we may feel about our spiritual progress. We read one of the most violent conflict stories in the life of Jesus. He has been in trouble with the Pharisees for seeming to sit lightly to some of the details of the Law, and privileging compassion above ritual observance. The final conflict with the Jewish and Roman authorities is still to come. Now he faces a hostile crowd, made increasingly angry by his words. The good news which he proclaims is too much for their understanding, too liberating for minds conditioned to living in a closed system of belief and practice. They call him a Samaritan, one from the north country, heretical in belief and separated from orthodox Jewry. The insult is ironical to those who know the Gospel stories: how Jesus spoke intimately and patiently to a Samaritan woman, how a Samaritan was the only one of ten cleansed lepers to return thanks, and a travelling Samaritan is the righteous man in one of the best-loved parables. They accuse him of being demonically possessed, hearing his saving words as the voice of evil. The climax comes when he speaks the words, 'I am', the sacred name of God given to Moses. In the Fourth Gospel Jesus uses the phrase several times to declare his truth, but the words of authority seem to be words of blasphemy. The penalty is stoning, but Jesus evades his enemies, not from fear but because his time is not yet come. The last and greatest conflict still lies ahead. He is to die at the time of Passover, the sacrificial lamb now is both victim and Saviour. He is to die publicly, a spectacle to the hostile and indifferent, a curiosity to the passing bystander, overwhelming grief to those who have loved him dearly and must suffer the anguish of thinking they have lost their Master for ever, judged by his own people and by the harsh law of a world power. For those who will listen to his teaching, he has fulfilled the promises of God to the people of the Covenant, and opened a new promise of salvation and eternal life. We who have believed and claim that promise must now follow in faith to the foot of the cross. Perhaps in Passiontide we shall pray especially for those who reject or fail to understand the saving words of our Lord. Let us so pray in love, with no sense of our own righteousness, acknowledging our failures. We keep our eyes upon the cross which always stands above our public worship, whether the occasion is joyful or sorrowful.

Blessed Lord, in whom alone we have the promise of eternal life, keep me ever mindful of thy Passion, the suffering through which I may receive salvation.

As we approach more distinctly to the commemoration of our Lord's Passion, the one great object of the Church, as set forth in today's Gospel, is to show us that the cause of His rejection by the Jews was the confession of His Godhead. It on this that they seek to slay Him as guilty of death, by taking up stones, as in the fulfilment of the Law. It is this which afterwards, at the time of His death, comes forward in a very prominent manner, as in that great declaration before the High Priest on which He was condemned to die, and delivered up to the Gentiles. Thus the Gospel for today already prepares the way for His Passion, as showing that in that 'contradiction of sinners against Himself' which He 'endured' throughout, the one great culminating point, and the ultimate cause of His condemnation was this. This was the truth which He kept, as it were, under a veil in the usual reserve of His teaching, gradually disclosing the same rather by His works than His words.

Isaac Williams (1802–1865) *Sermons* 1855

The Sunday Next before Easter
Matthew 27.1–54

This is a day of mixed feelings. Best known to us as Palm Sunday. It begins with a procession, carrying branches or palm crosses, perhaps even accompanied by a donkey, and leads into the beginning of Holy Week and our spiritual journey towards the cross. The Gospels for each day this week are long, and do not include the triumphal entry which Palm Sunday commemorates and which is the Gospel for the First Sunday in Advent. We will select a thought from each of the daily readings which may help in our meditations on the Passion. Matthew's account of the trial of Jesus makes it clear that it was a communal voice which demanded the crucifixion. The Roman judge was strangely moved by Jesus, and his wife was so distressed by a dream that she tried to intervene – unusual boldness for a wife of that time. The centurion at the cross was moved to say, 'Truly, this was the Son of God.' It is sometimes suggested that those who shouted 'Hosanna' now turned to shouting, 'Crucify him'. It would be a sad comment on the fickleness of human opinion, though it is more likely that the crowd at the trial was an unruly mob assembled by the Jewish authorities. Whoever they were, they rejected the good and holy, and chose a man who had done much wrong. Let us at all costs avoid the cruel smear which their demand allowed the Church to cast upon the Jewish people for centuries. Wrongdoing, false choices, may be collective; there are sinful individuals in every oppression, every persecution, every genocide. We have the power to do good or to do evil, to make the right or the wrong choice. Many a popular Barabbas has been accepted at the expense of those who speak uncomfortable truths. We are all guilty, all complicit in the dark side of human nature. We have all made wrong choices, sometimes through ignorance, sometimes consciously, with deliberate knowledge of what we were doing. It is the sin which is described in story form in Genesis, the primal sin of disobedience which tainted our human nature and could be redeemed only by the supreme sacrifice of the God whose command was

61

broken. Through this week we can think of some of the times when the wrong way seemed so attractive that we followed it. We share the guilt of fallen humanity, yet there is no place for holding feelings of guilt which make our lives negative. Former sins may be remembered with sadness and new resolve, but we lack humility if we continue to dwell on repented and cancelled sin. Let us remember without despair, without morbid dwelling on the past, but rather giving thanks for the love of God which does not let us go when we fail and for our sakes gave the Son into the power of cruel men.

Gentle Saviour, who didst suffer for my sins and the sins of the whole world, grant me at this holy time the spirit of true reverence, and in all my life hereafter grace to choose what is good and reject what is evil.

It was but now their sounding clamours sung,
    'Blessed is he that comes from the Most High.'
And all the mountains with Hosanna rung;
And now, 'Away with him – away!' they cry,
And nothing can be heard but 'Crucify!'
    It was but now the crown itself they gave,
    And golden name of King unto him gave;
And now, no king but only Caesar they will have.

Giles Fletcher (?1585–1623) 'Crucify Him', *Christ's Victory*

Monday before Easter
Mark 14.1–72

Mark is the shortest of the four Gospels, often brief and economical in the narrative but sometimes giving a detail which the others lack. In the passage for today it alone among the accounts of events in the Garden of Gethsemane, refers to the young man who fled away naked: some think that this was Mark himself, a personal signature of his witness. Today we read of how Jesus was betrayed, deserted and denied by his closest friends, triple suffering before the horror of the cross. We know little about Judas, who seems to have been the only Judean among the Galilean disciples. He is always referred to as the traitor, the betrayer. His motive is uncertain, whether simply for money or because in some way he was disappointed with what Jesus was doing. He could have been a Zealot, a Jewish nationalist, hoping for positive revolt against Roman rule. His kiss as a sign for the arrest of his Master is particularly cruel. Peter, James and John, always a special group among the Twelve, simply fall asleep and do not support Jesus in his agony. When they wake, it is Peter who is singled out for warning against temptation – Peter who has always been the first to speak and who so recently declared that he would go with Jesus even to death. He runs away with the others, gains courage to follow, and then falls away when the situation is threatening. His denial becomes more vehement, ending in anger and cursing as he defends himself. His promise of loyalty even to death is broken, but all the Twelve have affirmed the same during their last meal of fellowship, the precious time when Jesus has given them a new commandment, a promise sealed in his body and blood. The lessons for today are clear enough, to be accepted with repentance for the past and resolve for the future. We have not been true to our Christian duty when there seemed to be some personal advantage in setting it aside. We have turned away from our Lord when we were weary or distracted. We have denied our faith in the face of ridicule or hostility, a situation facing many Christians today. Yet Peter's offence can be a cause not for despair but for hope. He becomes a witness of the resurrection, he is thrice tested, then accepted and given a new mission on the shore of Lake Galilee where he was first called to follow Jesus. He receives the Holy Spirit with the others at Pentecost, immediately begins the proclamation of the gospel, becomes a leader of the new church in Jerusalem, and by tradition Bishop of Rome where he suffers martyrdom. Never was the possibility of true repentance and the pardoning love of God more clearly shown. Out of

the darkness of Holy Week there shines comfort and assurance
for the repentant sinner. May the love of Jesus reign in us and
keep us faithful.

*Blessed Lord, betrayed, deserted, denied, pardon the many times
when I have broken my vows of faith and obedience: keep me
close to thy presence, and let me never again fail thee or forsake
thee.*

The Saviour looked on Peter. Ay, no word,
No gesture of reproach! The heavens serene,
Though heavy with armed justice, did not lean
Their thunders that way! the forsaken Lord
Looked only on the traitor. None record
What that look was, none guess: for those who have seen
Wronged lovers loving through a death-pang keen,
Or pale-cheeked martyrs smiling to a sword,
Have missed Jehovah at the judgment –
'I never knew this man' – did quail and fall, call.
And Peter, from the height of blasphemy
As knowing straight that God – turned free
And went out speechless from the face of all,
And filled the silence, weeping bitterly.

I think that look of Christ might seem to say
'Thou Peter! art thou then a common stone
Which I at last must break my heart upon
For all God's charge to his high angels may
Guard my foot better? Did I yesterday
Wash thy feet, my beloved, that they should run
Quick to deny me 'neath the morning sun?
And do thy kisses, like the rest, betray?
The cock crows coldly. Go, and manifest
A late contrition, but no bootless fear!
For when thy final need is dreariest,
Thou shalt not be denied, as I am here;

My voice to God and angels shall attest,
Because I know this man, let him be dear.'

Elizabeth Barrett Browning (1806–1861) 'The Saviour Looked
on Peter', *Poems*

Tuesday before Easter
Mark 15.1–39

In their narratives of the Passion, among all the people, good and
bad, whose names are remembered for their part in fulfilling the
loving purpose of God, one man makes a brief appearance and
is seen no more. Simon of Cyrene was pressed by soldiers, with
the authority of the Roman rulers of Palestine, to take the cross
from the wounded shoulders of Jesus and follow in the way to
Calvary. Whether the soldiers had a rare moment of compassion
or, more likely, were afraid that Jesus would die on the road and
complicate their routine, they picked on a bystander who perhaps
looked strong enough for the burden. Simon was not an inhabit-
ant of Jerusalem: he came from Cyrene, a region in what is now
Libya. He was probably a Jew of the Dispersion, those living outside Palestine, many of whose congregations Paul visited on his
travels. He would have come to Jerusalem for the Passover. Of
the three Evangelists who mention Simon, only Mark names him
as 'the father of Alexander and Rufus'. There is a tradition that
the power of the cross brought about a change in Simon, and
he became a Christian. There is no evidence for this attractive
idea, though the naming of his sons does suggest that they were
known in the early Church. Whatever the conclusion, we can picture Simon struggling on the way, with mutinous thoughts about
the power of Rome, and the convicted man who had brought
this labour upon him. What his part in the story tells us without
question is that ordinary people, seemingly unremarkable in their
daily lives, may be caught up and given a small part in the great
drama of God's purpose. Any of us may be called for a service

which seems irksome and not very important, but in which we are chosen to be used. We may speak of some lasting trouble, or some comparatively slight annoyance, as 'a cross which we have to bear'. These are thoughtless words about something which is at the heart of the Gospel message. Jesus had said to those who were drawn to his teaching that each one must 'deny himself, and take up his cross, and follow me' (Mark 8.34). That which became a literal command for Simon is a continual challenge to all Christians. Not on a hot, dusty road in Palestine, but in home or office, hospital or church, there may be something to be borne for the sake of the One who bore the ultimate burden of human sin. When the call comes, do we walk away and lay down the burden of the cross which Jesus bore for us? The death of our Lord for all his children links us one to another. Paul writes, 'Bear ye one another's burdens, and so fulfil the law of Christ' (Galatians 6.2). Jesus himself said of the various works of mercy, 'Inasmuch as ye have done it unto the least of these my brethren, ye have done it unto me' (Matthew 25.40).

Lord, let me remember thy suffering on the way to Calvary, and be ready to recover the burden of others for the sake of the love which brought salvation to the world.

Now I saw in my dream, that the highway up which Christian was to go, was fenced on either side with a wall, and that wall was called Salvation. Up this way, therefore, did burdened Christian run, but not without great difficulty, because of the load on his back. He ran thus till he came at a place somewhat ascending, and upon that place stood a cross, and a little below, in the bottom, a sepulchre. So I saw in my dream, that just as Christian came up with the cross, his burden loosed from off his shoulders, and fell from off his back, and began to tumble, and so continued to do, till it came to the mouth of the sepulchre, where it fell in, and I saw it no more. Then was Christian glad and lightsome, and said, with a merry heart, 'He hath given me rest by his sorrow, and life by his death.' Then he stood still awhile to look and wonder; for it was very surprising to him, that the sight of the cross should thus ease him of his burden. He looked therefore, and looked again, even till the springs that were in his head sent the waters down his cheeks.

John Bunyan (1628–1688) *The Pilgrim's Progress*

Wednesday before Easter
Luke 22.1–71

Luke's Passion Gospel takes us through the familiar story and gives us the fullest account of the eucharistic words and actions at the Last Supper. He also emphasizes the appointed time, the immediacy of all that is drawing the incarnate life of Jesus to the end. Throughout his ministry the Lord has been preparing for this hour, saying openly that his time has not yet come, evading those who would kill him. Now he tells his disciple plainly that this is his last meal with them, his last Passover when all obedient Jews were to eat the ritual meal and remember the liberation of Israel from Egypt. This Passover is the beginning of his suffering, liberation not for himself or for his people alone, but for the whole world. In Gethsemane he confronts the last temptation, the last chance to escape from human suffering by divine power. He accepts the challenge: the victory is won, for this is the hour of decision. In a last act of mercy he heals the servant's ear, the climax of many individual healings, the sign of spiritual healing for all who will come to him in faith. The evil closes in as he tells his enemies, 'This is your hour, and the power of darkness.' As the night moves into the terrible day, he makes the declaration which allows his judges to condemn him. In the Greek of the New Testament there is a word, '*kairos*', which means 'time' not in the sense of its general passing but as a particular and important point. It is often used in the Gospels and Epistles to indicate a significant time in the eternal purpose of God. This is the time, the day, the hour, divinely appointed for the death of the Son of God in the flesh and the beginning of a new dispensation for human nature redeemed. Has Lent taught us to be more aware of God's purpose for each of us, to be alert to his calling in the little things as well as the great? For everyone there will be more than one *kairos* when we must respond as we are guided. For the individual, the Church, the nation, there are moments of decision. Even in the most seemingly uneventful life, there are continual choices to be made. The freedom of human will which allows us to sin also opens us to the possibility of something well done for God. The image of a crossroads, of the parting of ways where one must decide which way to turn, is found in the tales and legends of all nations. The victory was won on Calvary, but the conflict continues. Jesus took the road to the cross for the sake of us all, and gave a new meaning to our freedom. There are still choices to be made between good and evil; to accept the hour of darkness or the hour of light.

Lord whose steadfast love for the whole world didst lead thee to death on the cross, keep me ever alert to thy calling and ready to perform thy will at the time appointed for my obedience.

Once to every man and nation
    Comes the moment to decide,
In the strife of truth with falsehood,
    For the good or evil side:
Some great cause, God's new Messiah,
    Offering each the bloom or blight;
And the choice goes by for ever
    'Twixt that darkness and that light.

Then to side with truth is noble,
    While we share her wretched crust,
Ere her cause bring fame and profit,
    And 'tis prosperous to be just;
Then it is the brave man chooses,
    While the coward stands aside,
Doubting in his abject spirit
    Till his Lord is crucified

James Russell Lowell (1819–1891) 'The Present Crisis'

Thursday before Easter

Luke 23.1–49

On this day we think particularly of the Last Supper, when Jesus ate and talked with his closest friends on the eve of his Passion. We may like to read again the verses in yesterday's Gospel which tell of it, and consider the Epistle for today. But this day's Gospel also continues on our meditation on the cross. It is known as Maundy Thursday, recalling the *mandatum*, 'commandment', to the disciples, 'That ye love one another, as I have loved you' (John 13.34). Luke, whose witness contains many tender episodes and parables, gives us three precious examples of the love of Jesus continuing to the end. Luke always shows special regard for the women who came into the life of Jesus, and he relates how some of the women lamented on the road to Calvary. Jesus tells them not to weep for him but to prepare themselves for the sorrow that would fall upon them and their children with the coming destruction of Jerusalem. He has compassion for their sorrow; as he had wept with those who were mourning the death of Lazarus. Some of these women may have followed him in his ministry and been with him at the end, as the reading tells us. As he is being nailed to the cross he prays for mercy towards those who are killing him, pleading their ignorance of the terrible reality of what they are doing, inflicting a dreadful death on the Son of God. In his last agony he accepts the repentance of one of the men crucified with him, and assures him of peace and joy to come. Dying with Jesus will be the entry to eternal life with him. There are so many things for our devotions at this time. Can we hope by grace to imitate our Lord in sympathy for others, forgiveness for those who have wronged or hurt us, true repentance for our own sins and ungrudging reconciliation whenever it is offered? Too often we read the familiar Gospel stories, perhaps with care and devotion, but not fully engaging with their reality in the event and their continual meaning for us. The record of the Passion must surely draw us into a deeper contemplation, a sharing of that which in one sense we can never share, yet which draws us just as we are, unworthy yet allowed to come into the reality of that great divine sacrifice. As we try, however feebly, to share with Jesus in his suffering, we can try also to show the love which he commanded, and bestowed to the end. In the simple words of Julian of Norwich, 'Love was his meaning.'

Gracious Lord, whose love never faileth, who didst care for the women of Jerusalem, forgive thy murderers and receive the penitent thief, may I honour thy suffering by love to thee and to all who touch my life in this world.

Have, have ye no regard, all ye
Who pass this way, to pity me
Who am a man of misery?

A man both bruis'd, and broke, and one
Who suffers not here for mine own
But for my friends' transgression?

Ah! Sion's Daughters, do not fear
The Cross, the Cords, the Nails, the Spear,
The Myrrh, the Gall, the Vinegar,

For Christ, your loving Saviour, hath
Drunk up the wine of God's fierce wrath;
Only, there's left a little froth,

Less for to taste, than for to shew
What bitter cups had been your due,
Had He not drank them up for you

Robert Herrick (1591–1674) 'His Saviour's Words', *Works*

Good Friday
John 19.1–37

On this most solemn day of the year we are drawn into the heart of our faith, the sacrificial death of Jesus which was made once for all, and conveys his love in every moment of time. We shall probably be taking part in public worship, perhaps a procession of witness, but there will be much private and silent meditation on the cross. Every verse in the Gospel for the day has deep meaning, drawing the reader into some aspect of all that happened on Calvary. The divine anguish, the suffering accepted by God made vulnerable to all the ills of this world, is beyond our comprehension. We can only gaze and wonder, fixing our eyes upon the cross and trying to imagine ourselves alone with Jesus in the last hours of his incarnation. There is nothing now but silence and sorrow, praise and wonder, all mingled in our hearts. Yet there is something to link us with the timeless through the centuries that have passed. This was not a mythical event, a struggle of gods and heroes in which mortals had no part. The hill of Calvary stood outside a busy city where people were living their various lives, knowing their own joys and sorrows. During this week we have reflected on many of the people who played their part in those last days. Some have only one mention in the Gospels – Simon of Cyrene, Pilate, the Roman soldiers among them. Others, especially the disciples, had been close to the ministry of Jesus, all of them witnessing that the supreme act of God was done by human agents, by people who did not fully understand. We read of those who were with Jesus to the end, who stood at the foot of the cross until he died. His blessed mother, Mary Magdalene, his aunt the wife of Cleophas and the Beloved Disciple, traditionally John, author of the Fourth Gospel, offering their helpless grief for the man they loved. We can try to share something of their pain, as we dare not try to feel the whole suffering of Jesus; physical pain, the mockery of his enemies, the terrible cry of desolation recorded by the other Evangelists, as his human strength ebbed away and he felt himself forsaken. When she presented her son in the Temple, Mary was told that a sword would pierce her own heart, and now the anguish had come. All of them thought that their dear one was leaving them for ever. The human love which had drawn them close to incarnate deity was strong until the end. In that hour of sorrow, Jesus still had thought for his mother, and his friend took her into his care. God came as a man, to live as a man, to be a son, a teacher, a friend, to die as a man. On that fatal hill, human love was for ever sanctified.

Blessed Lord who as on this day didst suffer the death of the cross
for my sins and the sins of the whole world, accept my humble
thanks for the love of family and friends, and grant that I may
share with them the blessing of thine eternal love.

Now I bid you consider that that Face, so ruthlessly smitten, was
the Face of God Himself; the Brows bloody with the thorns, the
sacred Body exposed to view and lacerated with the scourge, the
Hands nailed to the Cross, and, afterwards, the Side pierced with
the spear; it was the Blood, and the sacred Flesh, and the Hands,
and the Temples, and the Side, and the Feet of God Himself,
which the frenzied multitude then gazed upon. This is so fearful
to thought, that when the mind first masters it, surely it will be
difficult to think of any thing else; so that, while we think of it,
we must pray God to temper it to us, and to give us strength to
think of it rightly, lest it be too much for us. Taking into account,
then, that Almighty God Himself, God the Son, was the Sufferer,
we shall understand better than we have hitherto the description
given of Him by the Evangelists; we shall see the meaning of His
general demeanour, His silence, and the words He used when he
spoke, and Pilate's awe at Him. Yes, we shall all of us, for weal
or for woe, one day see that holy Countenance which wicked
men struck and dishonoured; we shall see those Hands that were
nailed to the cross; that Side which was pierced. We shall see all
this; and it will be the sight of the Living God.

J. H. Newman (1801–1890) *Parochial and Plain Sermons*

Easter Even
Matthew 27.57–66

After the deep devotions and the long Gospel readings of the past
week, this is a day of rest, a liminal time between the season of
penance and the season of greatest rejoicing. The short reading
for today seems like an epilogue to the great drama which has

just been unfolded. Mary, mother of the Lord, and other grieving women, variously named by the Evangelists, witness the last
hasty rite of burial. Pilate, wanting to be rid of the troublesome
case, abruptly hands over responsibility to the Jewish authorities, who are still nervous – not believing in the coming resurrection but suspecting the disciples of planning to obtain the sacred
body. But the eleven remaining from the Twelve are silent, hiding
in their fear and remorse. The darkness which fell upon the land
in the dying hours of God Incarnate shrouds all that follows.
The burial is made urgently, without proper preparation, to be
completed before sunset on the eve of the Sabbath. The grieving women will come to complete the rites of death as the sun
begins to rise on the morning of the third day. Mary Magdalene
will come to look for the body of her Lord very early, while it
is still dark. Those who have been at the centre of the Passion
story seem now about to make their exit, and leave the scene to
silence and sorrow. A new figure appears, Joseph of Arimathea,
mentioned in all four Gospels. If we collate all that is written of
him, he was a rich man, a member of the Sanhedrin, who had not
concurred in the verdict against Jesus, a secret disciple who in
fear had concealed his full belief. Now he comes to do the last of
services, offering decent burial with a clean shroud and the tomb
which he had prepared for himself. The Fourth Gospel brings
Nicodemus, who had come to Jesus by night, as his companion.
In human terms, Joseph's love seems to be shown too late, an act
of charity rather than a confession of faith. But he is remembered
for his giving of that most sacred spot, the tomb of the incarnate
Lord, and pious legends followed him into the Christian story.
We may well pray today for the many believers who declare their
faith in the face of discrimination and persecution. We may think
of the times when we have been lukewarm in our witness, slow
in response to God's calling. This is a day for silent meditation,
considering the 40 days that have past, penitent but not obsessed
by our failures, joyful but not complacent for spiritual progress,
preparing for the new dawn. Love lies silent in the grave which
will not contain it.

Loving Lord, laid in the tomb, fill my heart with love towards
thee, bless and confirm my penitence for sin and my desire for
amendment, made in the weeks that have passed, grant me to
know the beauty of holiness to the end of my days here on earth,
and bring me to eternal life.

O blessed body! whither art thou thrown?
No lodging for thee, but a cold hard stone?
So many hearts on earth, and yet not one
      Receive thee?

Sure there is room without our hearts' good store;
For they can lodge transgressions by the score:
Thousands of toys dwell there, yet out of door.
      They leave thee.

But that which shows them large, shows them unfit.
Whatever sin did this pure rock commit,
Which holds thee now? Who hath indited it
      Of murder?

Where our hard hearts have took up stones to brain thee,
And missing this, most falsely did arraign thee;
Only these stones in quiet entertain thee,
      And order.

And as of old, the Law by heavenly art
Was writ in stone: so thou, which also art
The letter of the word, find'st no fit heart
      To hold thee.

Yet do we still persist as we began,
And so should perish, but that nothing can.
Though it be cold, hard, foul, from loving man
      Withhold thee.

George Herbert (1593–1633) 'O blessed Body', *Works*

Easter Day
John 20.1–10

Our picture of the first Easter morning is probably one of sunshine, beautiful surroundings and tremendous joy. What the Gospels describe is darkness just before dawn, shock, fear and bewilderment. For the Christian the empty tomb is a token of eternal hope; those who first came to it saw only a continuation of the horror they had known two days previously. It seemed as if their desire to render the last service to their Master had failed, that they would not see him again even in death, and that his enemies had completed their malice by taking away his body. The first to come on that morning were true to their characters as they had appeared in the Gospels: Mary Magdalene coming early, and urgent with a woman's love and desire to do what remained possible; Peter, impetuous, rushing into the tomb; the Beloved Disciple running eagerly to see for himself what Mary had told him, reverently hesitating, then entering and beginning to understand. The idea of seeing the truth, the light of revelation, is a theme throughout the Fourth Gospel. Jesus himself had said to them, 'I am the Light of the World.' This greatest of all truths, the ultimate wonder, had to be reached gradually and according to the capacity of those who received it. The first response was to go away, to return to the familiar comfort of home where they could ponder on what they had seen. When we adduce evidence for the truth of the resurrection, surely the negative first response is convincing. These were not people deluded by hope, expecting a miracle at that dark hour, but those who were yet to be given the grace of seeing and believing. The light shining in darkness of which John wrote in his Prologue was breaking through the darkness of the first dawn of the week. We rejoice today because we know the whole story. The appearances of the risen Lord soon to come, his presence in the Church, in the sacraments, and in our own spiritual experience. What seemed like the final loss was in truth the first morning of the new creation. This Sunday is indeed, above all others, the Lord's Day, the day of life. We are Easter people following those who first came to the tomb; who saw their Lord again, familiar yet gloriously transformed. As we have tried with faltering steps to walk with our Lord to Calvary, he walks beside us, our companion on every journey, our guest at every meal, our assurance in every moment of prayer. He will never leave us or forsake us. For our part we are to show forth, by our little light, a glimpse of the light which fills the whole world. May the living Christ reign in us today and for ever after.

Lord of all life, the hearts of thy people are glad as they rejoice in the glory of the resurrection. Accept my thanks for the gift of faith, and grant that the living Christ may fill me with faith, hope and joy this day and in all my days to come.

Most glorious Lord of life! that, on this day,
Didst make thy triumph over death and sin;
And, having harrowed hell, didst bring away
Captivity thence captive, us to win:
This joyous day, dear Lord, with joy begin;
And grant that we, for whom thou didest die,
Being with thy dear blood clean washed from sin,
May live for ever in felicity!
And that thy love we weighing worthily,
May likewise love thee for the same again;
And for thy sake, that all like dear didst buy,
With love may one another entertain:
So let us love, dear Love, like as we ought;
Love is the lesson which the Lord us taught.

Edmund Spenser (c 1552–1599) Sonnet 78, *Amoretti*

Monday in Easter Week
Luke 24.13–35

A new character appears in the story, Cleopas, whose wife was standing at the foot of the cross (John 19.25). It is a reminder that there were more disciples of Jesus than the named Twelve, and that there were others distressed and puzzled on that first day of the week. After reading of the empty tomb, we learn how the risen Christ appeared in bodily form, walking and eating like any man, not immediately recognized by his closest friends, able to disappear from sight. For all his teaching about his coming Passion and resurrection, Jesus still found that his followers were not understanding, unable to grasp the meaning of the past three days. The two who walked with him to Emmaus were given more instruction on the way. Like the lepers who were cleansed as they were walking towards Jerusalem, these two were enlightened while they were walking away from it and the trouble which they had known there. Here was the Messiah himself, explaining to them the prophecies of his coming; here the old wisdom was opening into the new age of salvation. They knew that this was someone very special who could touch their inmost being, but the full revelation would come only through their response. Moved perhaps by the love which they had learned from their Master, they offered him hospitality when they reached their destination, even in their sorrow having concern for a wandering stranger. As they sat to eat together, realization came in the fourfold action of taking, blessing, breaking and giving bread – what Jesus had done in the feeding miracles and at the Last Supper. It is Luke alone who gives us this story, and it is he who has the fullest Gospel account of the words and actions of Jesus with the bread and wine on that night. In the room at Emmaus and later that evening, the basic duties and privileges of the new Church were revealed: divine teaching and sacramental assurance. Through the centuries, Christians have heard the word and taken part in the holy mysteries. Strengthened by our Lenten devotions, we can make our Easter resolve to dedicate ourselves again to the service of God, more attentive to the teaching, more faithful in our sacramental life. With the eye of faith, we find the Lord at his holy table, as his companions found him in the breaking of bread. Unseen but deep in our inmost being, he walks with us, sits with us, offers us his grace. Do we always remember to ask him to abide with us, do we see him in the need of the stranger?

Risen Lord, who art always close to those who put their trust in thee and accept thy love, give me grace to know thee in word and sacrament and to walk with thee beside me until the end of my journey.

St Mark says he appeared to the two disciples who were going into the country, to Emmaus, 'in another form'. St Luke, who gives the account more at length, says, that while He talked with them their hearts burned within them. And it is worth remarking, that the two disciples do not seem to have been conscious of this at the time, but on looking back, they recollected that as having been, which did not strike them while it was. 'Did not,' they said, 'Did not our heart burn within us, while He talked with us by the way, and while he opened to us the Scriptures?' But at the time their hearts seem to have been holden (if we may use the expression) as well as their eyes. They were receiving impressions, but could not realise to themselves that they were receiving them; afterwards however, they became aware of what had been. Let us observe, too, when it was that their eyes were opened; here we are suddenly introduced to the highest and most solemn Ordinance of the Gospel, for it was when He consecrated and brake the Bread that their eyes were opened. There is evidently a stress laid on this, for presently St Luke sums up his account of the gracious occurrence with an allusion to it in particular. 'They told what things were done in the way, and how He was known of them in breaking of bread.'

J. H. Newman (1801–1890) *Catholic Sermons*

Tuesday in Easter Week
Luke 24.36–48

The Gospel for Monday is continued, with another reminder that there were more disciples than the inner group who had followed Jesus. The mention of 'the eleven' at the end of the previous passage is a sad comment on the loss of Judas from the fellowship of the Twelve. They are still frightened, wondering if the malice of authority will pursue them, not convinced by the appearance of the Lord to Simon Peter. Their first reaction to his sudden coming is the horror of a dead man's ghost, an apparition from beyond the grave come to haunt them, perhaps accuse them of their failures. In classical and Elizabethan tragedy, the appearance of a dead person is often one who comes to seek revenge on those responsible for the death, and these men had every reason to feel guilty of desertion, denial and concealment. Then the truth is revealed: this is indeed the Master they had loved and trusted, in the physical body that they knew so well, bearing the cruel marks of the cross, yet strangely changed, not confined by space. This was no ghost, but the loving Master they had known and failed, but who would never fail them or any who trusted in him. It is the assurance that there is no place for guilt in the life of faith. Deep sorrow for sin, confession, penitence, resolve for amendment – these are continually our need while we are in this world. But pardon is unqualified, reconciliation is complete, and not to accept it without reserve is to question God's mercy. These men knew that they had nothing to fear. To their joy, Jesus can still eat with them, share the meal fellowship which had seemed to end for ever on the eve of his Passion. The giving of fish relates to many things in the Gospel stories. Some of the first disciples were fishermen, called from their nets to be fishers of people, given the sign of a miraculous draught of fishes, repeated in one of the later resurrection appearances. Fish supplement the bread in the feeding miracles. The early Church took a fish as a symbol of faith, relating it to the Greek word for fish, *ichthys*, whose letters are the initials of the Greek words, 'Jesus Christ, Son of God, Saviour'. As thy eat together, Jesus continues his teaching, opening their eyes to further truth. But this is only the beginning. These men are to be witnesses to the faith far beyond Jerusalem. The word for 'witness' is also the word for 'martyr' and is so used later in the New Testament, of those from Stephen onwards who have suffered for Christ. Most of us are not called to the ultimate sacrifice, but we are all to be witnesses in our own time and place. May Christ be our unseen guest at every meal. The disciples thought at first that his return to them was too good to be true. Are we ever in danger of not being able to accept the magnitude of his endless mercy and love?

Blessed Lord, wounded for our sins, risen to open our way to eternal life, make me a faithful witness to thy truth, humbly accepting thy love, strengthened by the power of thy resurrection.

We must not think of Jesus Christ as behaving sometimes as God and sometimes as man like an actor appearing in two different roles. Whatever He did, He did as both God and man; in Him Godhead and manhood were indissolubly united in one perfect Person. This is illustrated, for example, by the appearance of Jesus to the disciples on the evening of Easter Day. He appears, suddenly, when the doors of the room were shut, and quiets their fears by showing them His hands and feet and side. He invites them to touch Him and eats before them. He also claims that the Scriptures have been fulfilled by His death and resurrection and He commissions them to preach forgiveness of sins in His Name. Here Docetism is rebuked – the theory that Jesus only seemed to be human. Here modern secularism is rebuked – the refusal to accept Jesus as God incarnate. But Jesus is showing himself as a complete Divine and human Person.

Edgar Dowse (1910–2007) *The Resurrection Appearances of our Lord*

The First Sunday after Easter
John 20.19–23

John here records the same experience as Luke told in the Gospel for last Tuesday, though with some differences of content and emphasis. The fear of those who had come together on that evening is made clear from the beginning. They do not need a supposed ghost to frighten them: they meet behind closed doors to hide from their enemies. Jesus in his risen body is not kept out by human defences; he comes among them, and they are joyful when they see him. As in Luke's account he shows them his wounds, but here there is attention also to his side, the wound of the spear thrust into his heart, the last symbolic rejection of his love. He greets the assembled group with the word 'Peace', the traditional Jewish word for welcome and assurance. It was the promise of the angels to the shepherds in Bethlehem, the word that stilled the storm on the Sea of Galilee, the promise of the last evening when he said, 'Peace I leave with you, my peace I give unto you. Not as the world giveth give I unto you.' Now indeed it is not a worldly but a heavenly and eternal peace which has come into the world. He still breathes as a man, but in his breath is the gift of the Holy Ghost, who will come with great signs at Pentecost. Here it is a quiet bestowal, a private commissioning of those who are being sent out to proclaim the good news. Luke tells of the same commandment to bear witness, but John adds the power to hear and absolve repented sins. Both word and sacrament are to be the privilege and the duty of his chosen representatives, then and in time to come. Frightened men receive courage to go out and face their enemies, to take the message to strange people and distant lands. In that room fear became assurance, sorrow turned to joy. The way is opened for the teaching of the apostles and their successors, the missionary journeys of Paul and of generations after him who would proclaim the gospel in the darkest places. Ordinary people, disregarded by the standards of the world, would be given power to serve the Church that was now beginning its formation. In that room fear became assurance, sorrow turned to joy. Let us pray that our doors shall always be open to the Lord who loves us and seeks us wherever we are.

O thou who art my Lord and my God, open my heart to take thee into my life. Grant me the blessing of thy peace, the assurance of thy presence, and the comfort of the Holy Ghost, ever guiding thy Church into the way of truth.

We were not by when Jesus came;
    But round us, far and near,
We see His trophies, and His name
    In choral echoes hear.
    In a fair ground our lot is cast,
    As in the solemn week that past,
    While some might doubt, but all adored,
Ere the whole widow'd Church had seen her risen Lord.

Then, gliding through th' unopening door,
　　Smooth without step or sound,
'Peace to your souls,' He said – no more –
　　They own Him, kneeling round.
　　Eye, ear, and hand, and loving heart,
　　Body and soul in every part,
　　Successive made His witnesses that hour,
Cease not in all the world to show His saving power.

For all thy rankling doubts so sore,
　　Love thou the Saviour still,
Him for thy Lord and God adore,
　　And ever do His will.
　　Though vexing thoughts may seem to last,
　　Let not thy soul be quite o'ercast; –
　　Soon will He show thee all His wounds, and say,
'Long have I known thy name – know thou My face alway.'

John Keble (1792–1866) 'St Thomas's Day'

The Second Sunday after Easter
John 10.11–16

The Gospel readings now return to earlier times when the Passion and resurrection were being foretold. When Jesus speaks of himself as a shepherd, we might say that the word gives a good feeling to a modern reader. We think of shepherds as generally good people, devoted workers in all weathers, with care and concern for their sheep. In the world of the New Testament shepherds had a different image, living in their own groups, on the fringes of society. They may not have been highly esteemed by society, but they deserved more respect than they received. Shepherds in Palestine were working not in enclosed fields but in plains and mountains, close to the wilderness, land in which savage animals prowled. When David was a shepherd, before he overcame Goliath and later became king, he was not a gentle, timid boy. He pursued and killed predators who stole a lamb from his flock (1 Samuel 17.34). Now a greater one than David is here, ready to do battle not against animals but against human and supernatural enemies. In this short discourse, Jesus twice speaks of himself as the good shepherd, one who loves his flock and will protect them even at the cost of his own life. His desire is not just for the survival of his human flock, but that they shall be brought to understand and accept the infinite love of God and be gathered into the new kingdom which is already among them. It is a call for the conversion of the human race, and also for the united fellowship of all who deem themselves Christians, a condition which is coming nearer but is still far from complete; it is a call for us all to be more zealous in the cause of ecumenism. The call is emphasized in the Greek text, where the words for 'fold' and 'shepherd' are the same, with only a difference in the grammatical gender. The Church and its Lord are one. There is also a warning, as relevant now as ever, against those who profess their love and duty with regard to how it may profit them, and who fall away in difficulty and danger. The ravening wolf has many shapes, many ways of testing our faith. Those who first heard these words of Jesus did not fully understand that his life was truly to be laid down for his sheep. We who know the whole story must rejoice in it, and honour it with our obedience.

Loving shepherd, constant even unto death for those who have no strength of their own, no hope but in thee, keep me faithful in this world, shield me from its dangers, and at the last gather me into thy heavenly fold.

Lead me to mercy's ever-flowing fountains;
For Thou my Shepherd, Guard, and Guide shalt be;
I will obey Thy voice, and wait to see
Thy feet all beautiful upon the mountains.
Hear, Shepherd! – Thou for Thy flock art dying,
O, wash away these scarlet sins, for Thou
Rejoices at the contrite sinner's vow.
O, wait! – to Thee my weary soul is crying,

Wait for me! – Yet why ask it, when I see,
With feet nailed to the cross, Thou'rt waiting still for me!

H. W. Longfellow (1807–1882) 'The Good Shepherd'

The Third Sunday after Easter
John 16.16–22

This is part of the passage known as the Farewell Discourse, the words which Jesus spoke to his disciples on the eve of his Passion. They had gathered for what was to be the Last Supper, and when he had finished his teaching they went out together to the Garden of Gethsemane, to his arrest, trial, condemnation and crucifixion. Christians ever since that time have found some of Jesus' deepest meaning and greatest comfort in these chapters. He has washed his disciples' feet, the humble act of a household slave, and then resumed the authority of their Master and teacher, the Son of God. The mystery of the incarnation is enfolded in that sequence. For a while he lets them talk among themselves, anxiously questioning what he has already said, which seems to be beyond their understanding. Then he speaks of what is soon to come: the malicious pleasure of his enemies, exercising their temporal power. His friends will suffer deep sorrow for a short time, and then be filled with a great joy. The warning and the promise are too much for them to take in. Jesus assures them, 'I will see you again', and this time their joy will be complete, there will be no loss. The idea of childbirth as a time of suffering followed by great joy is used in the Old Testament to tell how God gives new life, to the individual or to the nation. In another meeting by night, Jesus had said to Nicodemus, 'Ye must be born again.' Nicodemus did not understand, and as the accounts of the resurrection morning show, the disciples also were bewildered and the words of promise were not understood, the assurance was not accepted, until Jesus came among them in his new but familiar form. When he could eat and drink with them again, continue his teaching, and prepare them for what was yet to come, they could receive with joy the message that runs through the Bible from beginning to end: that the promises of God are not like human promises, liable to be broken, but are sure to be fulfilled. At the Last Supper the disciples departed in sorrow and fear; at the ascension they departed in hope and wonder. We continue sometimes to be uncertain about God's unfailing grace and pardon. We might be tempted to think that the disciples who had been so close to Jesus give us a precedent, until we remember that we know the whole story, and at this Easter season above all others our lives should be filled by the risen Christ.

Saviour God, thou hast promised new birth to those who trust in thee; open my heart to receive thee, increase my faith in thy promises, guide my steps day by day on the path of eternal life.

Yield yourselves to the Lord, that is, as his servants, give up the dominion and government of yourselves to Christ. Pray that he put you to whatsoever work he pleaseth. Servants, as they must do their master's work, so they must be for any work their master has for them to do: they must not pick and choose, this I will do, and that I will not do; they must not say this is too hard, or this is too mean, or this may be well enough, let alone. Good servants, when they have chosen their master, will let their master choose their work, and will not dispute his will, but do it.

John Wesley (1703–1791) Methodist Covenant Service

The Fourth Sunday after Easter
John 16.5–14

In this part of the Farewell Discourse, Jesus is teaching his disciples to adjust to the present situation and prepare for what is to come. They must understand the centrality of the cross in God's plan for the redemption of the human race, and when it has been accomplished they will need to learn many things before they are enabled to go out and spread the good news. At this moment they are confused and troubled, not wanting to accept the parting which is to come. They are not yet ready for the fullness of truth, and this is something to remember when we find it hard to discern what God is saying to us. Jesus knew that the time of fullness had not come. Surely in his mercy and love he knows when present troubles turn us away from the demands of our faith, and gently draws us back to himself. What follows in the discourse has some difficulties. 'Comforter' translates a Greek word which has the sense of an advocate, an adviser and defender in a legal case. The word 'comfort' itself, as elsewhere in the King James Version of the Bible, means to encourage and strengthen rather than to put at ease. The Holy Spirit will not come cosily, but in a mighty wind and tongues of fire. What the Comforter will do is also a little difficult to express, but essentially the ideas of this world will be proved wrong, regarding the uniqueness and perfection of our Lord, of his oneness with the Father, and the false values created by the evil in this world. The teaching is a preparation for the coming of the Holy Spirit at Pentecost, the completed revelation of God in unity and in Trinity. We have learned a great deal more than the disciples knew on that strange, terrible and glorious evening with their Lord. As Easter moves towards Pentecost, we turn away from the errors of this world, and open ourselves to the searching and assuring Light of God. There is in the Church a principle known as Reserve, a discipline of not speaking too freely and carelessly about religious matters, of having regard to the condition of the hearers. It does not silence the duty of continual witness, but it urges discretion and discernment. The doctrine of Reserve is still a warning and a guide for faithful Christians. It warns against any casual chat about the faith with people who sit lightly to it but like to feel that they have not lost a kind of Christian heritage which they associate with being British. The Christian faith is a message of joy, liberation, continual resurrection. It is also a faith that carries responsibilities of obedience both in the way of life and in private and public worship. Sometimes Jesus spoke to a crowd, sometimes to a few close followers; he is our pattern in this, as in all things.

Lord God, maker of all, sustainer of all, judge of all, thy ways are mysterious, yet they are opened by the power of the Holy Spirit.

Grant me discernment, keep me from error, dispel my darkness by the light of thy glory.

When the physical presence of the Lord was withdrawn at the Ascension, there remained on earth as fruit of His ministry no defined body of doctrine, no fully constituted society with declared aims and methods, but a group of men and women who had loved and trusted Him, and who by their love and trust and conviction of His Resurrection were united to one another. It was in this society that there came the experience of spiritual power, certainly a gift of God, and of inner compulsion to proclaim alike this gift of power and its source in the Life and Death and Resurrection of Jesus their Master. This society is a veritable Fellowship of the Holy Spirit. It is definable in terms of the Spirit; and the Spirit is definable in terms of it. To be a Christian is to confess Jesus as Lord, to have the Spirit, to be a member of the Church.

William Temple (1881–1944) *Christus Veritas*

The Fifth Sunday after Easter
John 16.23–33

The appointed time has come and Jesus prepares his disciples for the terrible events of the night and the next day, for Gethsemane and Calvary. Through all the years of their fellowship, through the miracles, the teaching and the prophecies, they have been slow to believe. At last their uncertainty is turned to assurance and they know that their beloved Master has indeed come forth from God, though they do not yet fully understand the full divinity in his humanity. He has taught them through stories and metaphors, symbols of shepherds and vineyards, but now they must be prepared for the plain truth, the full revelation. There is still much to be learned: their assurance must now begin, and be ready for things still unknown. The message now is of hope and coming joy, but there are also solemn warnings. Despite their new vows of faithfulness, in a few hours they will desert him, run away and leave him alone with his enemies.

They are trusting in their own excited feelings, believing that their own wills are strong enough. They must learn to find peace in the midst of a troubled world where they will be hated and persecuted by many in power. But there are great promises, for that little band and for all who in times to come will follow the same way that they have learned. The Father will hear prayers made in the name of the beloved Son. It is not enough for us to sign off our prayers with the formula 'Through Jesus Christ our Lord'. The prayer must be worthy of the ending, a fit offering in the name of the Lord who has opened this way for us. The disciples had received years of teaching; we have read the words and deeds of Jesus, have been given insight to read all Scripture in the light of his life, death and resurrection, have been given the interpretations and traditions of the Church. Yet we are not always faithful to our profession. The disciples were loving, but too sure of themselves. Complacency can be as great an enemy as doubt. It is worth reading the Gospel for today in connection with the Epistle, where James warns us to be doers of the word and not just hearers. As Jesus showed the love of the Father by healing and feeding as well as teaching, so we are to do the works of love, not to gain merit but as proof of our faith.

Father in heaven, source of all love and goodness, mercifully hear the prayers of thy people who call upon thee in this troubled world; accept my prayers in the name of Jesus Christ, my Lord and Saviour.

The life of prayer, in its widest and deepest sense, is our total life towards and in God; and therefore the most searching of all the purifying influences at work in us. It is the very expression of our spiritual status, a status at once so abject, and so august; the name of the mysterious intercourse of the created spirit with that Uncreated Spirit, in whom it has its being and on whom it depends. We are called, as the New Testament writers insist, to be 'partakers of the Divine Nature': and this is a vocation which shames while it transforms. So prayer may be, and should be, both cleansing and quickening: by turns conversation and adoration, penitence and happiness, work and rest, submission and demand. It should have all the freedom and variety, the depth and breadth of life; for it is in fact the most fundamental expression of our life.

Evelyn Underhill (1875–1941) *The Golden Sequence*

The Ascension Day
Mark 16.14–20

We need to read the beginning of the Acts of the Apostles for a full account of the ascension, but this short Gospel is of great value in exploring and accepting the message. It was written as an addition to the Gospel of Mark, which originally seems to have ended with the visit of the women to the tomb and the stark statement, 'they were afraid'. What we have here is a summary and compression of what followed the resurrection: how Jesus came to the disciples while they were eating, rebuked them for their continuing doubts and fears, gave them the great commission to tell the good news, and promised them help and power beyond their own strength. The writer looks onwards to the development of the early mission, probably referring to how Paul in Malta was attacked by a poisonous snake but was unharmed (Acts 28.3–6). It is a summary of the transition from the day of resurrection to the early years of the Church, almost like a reminder for the faithful of duties and assurances. The ascension itself is described in a few words, 'He was received up into heaven and sat on the right hand of God.' There is no detailed account, no mention of cloud or angels, but a plain statement that Jesus returned to his heavenly home, to be at one with the Father, having raised our fallen humanity to the greatest height. The ascension message is that human nature is no longer separated from God, no longer in exile, but given its place in the eternal glory. Bishop William Wand once said that after the ascension the human race is like a person standing up to the neck in water, safe because the head is above it. We are the heirs of the truth revealed to the apostles, and the duties to which they were commanded. We may have less spectacular signs to accompany our ministry, but the ministry is still here, no less than to play our part in the conversion of the world. The signs of our commission will be holy living, and the love which took Jesus through cross and resurrection to the glorious ascension.

My dear Lord, risen, ascended, glorified, who hast called thy faithful people to follow in the steps of the apostles, and to be messengers of thy kingdom, grant me grace to honour my calling, and to show forth thy praise with my lips and in my life.

Christ is now raised above the heavens; but he still experiences on earth whatever sufferings we his members feel. He showed that this is true when he called out from heaven: 'Saul, Saul, why do you persecute me?' And: 'I was thirsty and you gave me drink.' Why then do we not exert ourselves on earth so as to be with him already in heaven through the faith, hope and charity which unite us with him? Christ, while in heaven, is also with us; and we, while on earth, are also with him. He is with us in his godhead and his power and his love; and we, though we cannot be with him in godhead as he is with us, can be with him in our love, our love for him. He did not leave heaven when he came down to us from heaven: and he did not leave us when he ascended to heaven again. His own words show that he was in heaven while he was here: 'No one has ascended into heaven but he who descended from heaven, the Son of man who is in heaven.' He came down from heaven, then, in mercy; and it is he alone who has ascended, since we are in him through grace. This is why no one has descended but Christ, and no one but Christ has ascended: not that the dignity of the head is fused with the body but that the body in its unity is not separated from its head.

Augustine (354–430) *On the Ascension*

Sunday after Ascension Day
John 15.26–16.4

It is perhaps regrettable that Ascensiontide has been drawn into the Easter period rather than being honoured as a short season in itself. It is another period of waiting, for us as for the apostles, until the next part of the divine mystery is revealed. They had learned much from their Master during his incarnation, but there was more to come when they were filled with the power of the Holy Spirit. People sometimes ask how the Gospel writers could have known about the secret and solitary times of Jesus, like the temptation in the wilderness and the times of colloquy with Nicodemus and the Samaritan woman. Luke in Acts tells us that he spoke to them of things belonging to the kingdom of God in the 40 days between his resurrection and ascension, and Pentecost brought still more to their knowledge. We too have always more to learn, however regular our Bible study and spiritual reading, as we are granted more discernment of the truth. In this Farewell Discourse, Jesus also warns them of the suffering to come, to be prepared for persecution even to death. In those days his words and the memory of his presence will strengthen them, and we too must cling to our Lord in anxiety and adversity. The disciples had been faithful in the years since their calling, often failing to understand, showing impatience and jealousy, deserting Jesus in his hour of need, but at last made partakers of his resurrection. Some of us have been Christian believers for as long as we can remember, some have come more recently to faith, but by grace we have held fast to the hope that is in us and as Paul promises, Christ 'shall also confirm you unto the end' (1 Corinthians 1.8). However long or short our time of service, we shall never cease to hear the word of God if we open ourselves to him. The Comforter, our Advocate, is now called also 'the Spirit of Truth'. He is our guide, the source of our soul's health. Between Ascension and Pentecost we may meditate again on these words of Jesus. Infinite spiritual grace does not always protect us from worldly tribulation or from assaults on our physical and mental well-being. From trivial mockery to the final witness of a martyr's death, Christians may have to suffer in the love of their suffering Lord. Risen, ascended, glorified, he is with us in good times and in bad, in calm and in testing.

Gracious God from whom all truth proceeds, all power is given, guide me by the Spirit of Truth to know thy will, to be patient in adversity, and to persevere to the end in the faith which by thy grace I have received.

Here, as elsewhere in the Christian religion, what we find is not a complete novelty, but the revelation (in virtue of the divine indwelling) of the true significance of a familiar characteristic of human nature. The 'crowd' is not the mere sum of its component individuals; its temper is not the average of theirs. It is a collective unit, made one by the elimination for the moment of all in its members which is alien from its concern, and possessed of an eagerness in that concern greater than the individuals in isolation would feel. The concern may be loyalty, or patriotism, or revenge, or hatred; in the crowd it eliminates all else that might restrain or inhibit its expression. If the animating power is Christ, evoking loyalty as a means to the achievement of His purpose, then the 'crowd' becomes the Church, and is fitly called His Body.

William Temple (1881–1944) *Christus Veritas*

Whitsunday
John 14.15–31

Here again we must turn to the Acts of the Apostles for an account of what happened on the day of Pentecost. It is sometimes called 'the birthday of the Church', the beginning of the gospel message going out from Jerusalem to the whole world. The Holy Spirit is a gift to the Church, to uphold and inspire her for ever until the final consummation of God's purpose. We call on the power of the Holy Spirit in the sacraments, the blessing of baptism, the wonderful celebration of the Eucharist. That descent of the Holy Spirit that Jesus had promised to his disciples in his words to them after the Last Supper had come to pass. He had told them that there would be loss, a parting that seemed to be final, but a glorious return on the day of resurrection, with still more blessings to follow. The temporary severance had to come before the greater union, Christ ascended to the Father and a new life for redeemed humanity. The power of evil, the prince of this world, would seem to prevail. The battle had to be joined and the enemy would be overcome. Pentecost was the completion of the promises, and the start of a new era for the world which God had made. The disciples had learned many things, but there was much more needed to make them ready for their mission, and the Holy Spirit would continue and illuminate the teaching which their Master had given them when he walked on Earth. The Holy Spirit is also a gift to the world, which is a good world, God's world, though marred by human sin. The power of the apostles to speak in many tongues shows that divine grace is not confined to one nation or race. The Holy Spirit is at work in the world, often silently and unknown, but mighty in power. Jesus left them that evening with the promise of peace, the lovely word which had greeted his Nativity and would be spoken again in the upper room after the resurrection. It was a peace such as they had never known, not temporary, not subject to the strains and trials of each moment, but within them for ever. It was the peace that comes from the indwelling of the Holy Spirit in all who love the Lord. The Holy Spirit is also a gift to the individual who will receive the gift in faith and love. There is no need to seek for special powers or great signs. Anything that makes some Christians claim superiority over others in knowledge or favour is wrong. The power of the Holy Spirit appears in quiet lives, in the acceptance of the routine prescribed for us, as much as in any spectacular events in the history of the Church.

The proof of love, the assurance of peace, comes from obedience to God's word in faith and action. This is a day which continues to challenge us, and a day to give praise for the strength which we are given to meet the challenge. The Holy Spirit does not come to us in a mighty wind or in tongues of fire, but silently and secretly in our deepest selves. It is most wonderful to know that the Holy Spirit who descended on the apostles is indeed within us.

Holy Spirit of God, by whose guidance thy Church and all thy faithful people are led into the way of truth, enter into my inner being this day and all the days of my life, that I may know the peace that is not of this world, and come at last to the peace of heaven.

Consider that the Holy Ghost came down upon the Apostles in the shape of tongues, to signify that he came to make them fit preachers of his word, and to endow them with the gift of tongues, accompanied with the heavenly wisdom and understanding of the mysteries of God and all the gospel truths, to the end that they might be enabled to teach and publish, throughout the whole world, the faith and law of Christ! And these tongues were of fire, to signify how his divine Spirit sets those souls on fire in which he abides, inflaming them with divine love, consuming the dross of their earthly affections, putting them in a continual motion of earnest desires and endeavours to go forward from virtue to virtue as fire is always in motion, and carrying them upwards towards the God of Gods in his heavenly Zion, as the flame is always ascending upwards towards its element.

Richard Challoner (1691–1781) 1767 Whitsunday, *Meditations for Every Day*

Monday in Whitsun Week
John 3.16–31

These words of Jesus take us to the heart of the Christian message, the meaning of all that he did for our salvation. In pure, unmerited, unbounded love, God gave his son to live and die for us, that we might live in him for ever. It was the full measure of his goodness, the merciful exercise of his complete power. In the words of Julian of Norwich, 'Love was his meaning.' The image of that love which is used here is one that all can understand. We may need some help to take in the full sense of winegrowers or sowers, or even shepherds, but the difference between light and darkness has been human experience from the earliest years. The first word of creation as expressed in Genesis was, 'Let there be light.' The Bible begins with light, and ends in the book of Revelation with the eternal light of God in heaven when even the sun and moon are no longer needed. The psalms give us words to declare, 'The Lord is my light and my salvation' and to acknowledge our dependence on God, 'In thy light shall we see light' (Psalms 27.1; 36.9). In a passage often read as part of the preparation for Christmas, the prophet writes of the mercy of God towards Israel, 'The people that walked in darkness have seen a great light: they that dwell in the land of the shadow of death, upon them hath the light shined' (Isaiah 9.2). The light of God's glory breaks upon the shepherds who first hear of the birth of Jesus (Luke 2.8–9) and John tells of the coming of Christ, 'The true light' (John 1.9). The Holy Spirit, the particular subject of our devotion at this time, continues to pour into the world that light which Jesus brought to it in his incarnation. We rejoice in light, in its daily returning after the hours of darkness, making us able to see and relate to our world, but light is not always wholly welcome. It can show us too much, whether the disarray of a room neglected after the night before, or the dark reality of our sin. Sin is not just the sum of wrong deeds, continually repeated and continually repented. The ultimate and dreadful reality of sin is the conscious rejection of the light of the world in Christ, the choice to follow the evil instead of the good. We need courage to step into the light which searches and confronts us, but leads us into the right way. We can in our small way be bearers of that light if we live as those worthy of the name of Christians. 'Like a little candle, burning in the night', as an old hymn says, we are meant to add our little gleam to the all-pervading light of God. He will lead us from light to light, in this world and to life everlasting.

Holy Spirit of God, shed thy light upon me, that I may see the reality of my sinfulness, and may be led into the way of truth, and that the love which made and sustains all things may shine in me and bring me to everlasting life.

Dear Friends, prize your time and the love of the Lord to your souls above all things, and mind that Light in you that shows you sin and evil. Which checks you when ye speak an evil word, and tells you that you should not be proud, nor wanton, nor fashion yourselves like unto the world; for the fashion of this world passeth away. And if ye hearken to that, it will keep you in humbleness of mind, and lowliness of heart, and turn your minds within, to wait upon the Lord, to be guided by it; and bring you to lay aside all sin and evil, and keep you faithful to the Lord; and bring you to wait upon him for teaching, till an entrance thereof be made to your souls, and refreshment come to them from the presence of the Lord. There is your Teacher, the Light, obeying it; there is your condemnation, disobeying it.

George Fox (1624–1691) *Epistles* 17

Tuesday in Whitsun Week
John 10.1–10

We meet again the familiar image of the shepherd, so often found in the Bible, as a type of God's guiding and protecting love. Most of us, knowing little of a shepherd's work, may be surprised by the intimate relationship of which this passage tells. To the good shepherd, his sheep are not just a vague woolly crowd, but a number of individual creatures, each of them known to him by name. So it is in God's relationship with us. As the worship song says, 'He has the whole wide world in his hands' – but he also values and cares for each one of the men and women he has created, and knows them better than they can know themselves. He leads them through this world; for the Palestinian shepherd did not drive his sheep, but led them as Psalm 23 says, 'He leadeth me beside the still waters.' As the shepherd defends his sheep against thieves, God defends his people against false teachers and the attacks of those who make corrupt use of worldly power. There are many in our society who claim to be offering something for our benefit while they are really serving their own profit. We may think that sheep are rather stupid creatures, but they have the sense not to follow a stranger, who may have bad motives in calling them. Jesus is our leader, and our door through whom we enter into the kingdom of God, as the sheep enter the safety of the fold. The last verse of this passage is one of the most wonderful in the Bible: 'I am come that they might have life, and that they might have it more abundantly.' God's desire for us is fullness of life in this world, and eternal life thereafter. It is a sad error of some Christians to confuse purity of living with refusal of all enjoyment. When he walked among men and women, Jesus shared their rejoicing as well as their sorrow, until the over-righteous accused him of being too fond of pleasure. He leads us still into pleasant pastures, if we accept his grace. We pass through this world as a pilgrimage to eternal life in the perfect pastures of heaven, but we do not turn away from its good things. There is a Rabbinic saying that at the Day of Judgement people will be called to account for permissible pleasures deliberately refused in this life. Let us always be ready to hear the voice of the Good Shepherd, calling to each of us by the Holy Spirit in whom is the focus of our devotion at this season, to follow him, and to accept the richness of life redeemed. Surely it is of the nature of sin to refuse any part of the bounty of God.

Great Shepherd of thy sheep, open my ears to hear thy voice, guide my steps to follow thee, protect me from the evil powers that may afflict me, and fill me with the abundant life which comes through thy love.

Surely, the real difference that marks out Christianity from all other religions lies just here, in this robust acceptance of humanity in its wholeness, and of life in its completeness, as something which is susceptible of the divine. It demands, and deals with, the whole person, with his or her titanic energies and warring instincts; not, as did the antique mysteries, separating and cultivating some supposed transcendental principle in human beings, to the exclusion of all else. Christians believe in an immanent and incarnate God, who transfuses the whole of the life that He has created, and calls that life in its wholeness to union with Him. If this is so, then our belief should find its fullest expression in our prayer, and that prayer should take up, and turn towards the spiritual order all the powers of our mental, emotional and volitional life. Prayer should be the highest exercise of these powers for here they are directed to the only adequate object of thought, love and desire. It should, as it were, lift us to the top of our condition, and represent the fullest flowering of our consciousness, for here we breathe the air of the supernal order, and attain according to our measure to that communion with Reality for which we were made.

Evelyn Underhill (1875–1941) *The Essentials of Mysticism*

Trinity Sunday
John 3.1–15

Nicodemus was not a convinced follower of Jesus when he came to him by night. He seems to have been a man of devout nature, a member of the strictest followers of the Jewish Law. Like many people before and since, he was curious, drawn by what he had heard from others and wanting to see for himself. He came under cover of darkness, since his fellow-Pharisees were already in dispute with this new teacher and were beginning to work against him. He began with hopeful enquiry and ended with the revelation of new wonder. Nicodemus seems to have had a literal mind, totally confused by the idea of a grown man being born again, then given the message of spiritual rebirth, through the water of baptism and the indwelling of the Holy Spirit, truths which would in time be shown to the new Church of God. In the Greek text the word for 'wind' and 'spirit' are the same. It is not a humorous play on words but rather tells of the free-ranging and unseen work of the Holy Spirit filling the whole created world. The mystery of the Holy Trinity is figured here: the Son sent by the Father to take our human nature, the Spirit making his work of redemption effective in each individual believer. Nicodemus is told of the great sacrifice which brought that redemption when Jesus was lifted up on the cross, and the promise of eternal life. That promise has been fulfilled for us, for all Christians who know the fullness of God's purpose and have believed. Today we centre our devotions on the Holy Trinity, a mystery never to be fully grasped with our mortal minds, but fundamental to Christian belief. We declare our faith in God, Three in One and One in Three, at baptism, in blessing and absolution, at the beginning of sermons, in graces and private prayers. We may and should continually seek to understand more about our faith, but we must be prepared for some surprises, and respect the limits of human reason. Not intellectual curiosity, but praise and wonder must mark our worship. It seems that Nicodemus never told of his new faith while Jesus was living, but according to John he came with Joseph of Arimathea to lay his body to rest. It is never too late to offer the humble service of love.

Holy and glorious Trinity, whose mystery is revealed through grace and gives power to thy Church, pardon my doubts and my failures in faith, let me not trust in my unaided wisdom but sanctify my life and bring me into the kingdom of the newly born.

A certain faith is in some way the starting-point of knowledge; but a certain knowledge will not be made perfect, except after this life, when we shall see face to face. Let us therefore be thus minded, so as to know that the disposition to seek the truth is more safe than that which presumes things unknown to be known. Let us therefore so seek as if we should find, and so find as if we were about to seek. For 'when a man hath done, then he beginneth'. Let us doubt without unbelief of things to be believed; let us affirm without rashness of things to be understood: authority must be held fast in the former, truth sought out in the latter. As regards this question, then, let us believe that the Father, and the Son, and the Holy Spirit is one God, the Creator and Ruler of the whole creation; and that the Father is not the Son, nor the Holy Spirit either the Father or the Son, but a trinity of persons mutually interrelated, and a unity of an equal essence. And let us seek to understand this, praying for help from Himself, whom we wish to understand; and as much as He grants.

Augustine (354–430) *On the Holy Trinity*

First Sunday after Trinity
Luke 16.19–31

We begin the long sequence of Sundays after Trinity, called in the Common Worship lectionary 'Ordinary Time'. It is a season of longer days, and green vestments, quieter than the special observances of the preceding months. It is a time when we may feel that our devotions are less demanding, that we can rest in knowledge of rules faithfully observed. The first Sunday after Trinity immediately confronts us with a challenge, a reminder that Christianity is not a passive religion of purely spiritual duty, but one that demands practical obedience to the rule of love. From the mystery of the Holy Trinity, the Gospel leads us to a simple and demanding story of deprivation which is as familiar now as when it was told, witnessed around us every day. This is one of the most vivid stories that Jesus told, with details ranging from expensively coloured garments and scavenging dogs to the mystery of life after death. Like many of his parables, it is a tale of the complete reversal of expected human values. At other times he tells of equal pay for unequal work, more delight in one straying sheep than in 99 who behaved themselves, selling off all possessions to buy a single jewel. There will be some great surprises in the life to come, when everyone is seen through the all-knowing wisdom and judgement of God. This parable is not a denunciation of wealth in itself but of its selfish use. We are told, not that money is the root of all evil as it is often misquoted, but that 'the love of money is the root of all evil' (1 Timothy 6.10). The Epistle for today says that we cannot truly love God if we are not loving other people. Good works alone are not the way of salvation, but the atonement brought by the ultimate sacrifice of divine love calls for the response of good works as the gratitude and proof of faith. The rich man's brothers had the words of their Scripture to guide them into the right way. We have the words of the new Covenant, which tells us that One did indeed rise from the dead. Our privilege is greater, and our obligation is greater. The Gospel for today is a call to make good use of this long Trinity season, to fulfil in renewed lives the spiritual graces granted to us from Advent to Trinity Sunday. We are called to be more sensitive to the needs of others, emotional as well as physical, to do works of mercy as opportunity and circumstance offer. It seems that the rich man was beginning to think beyond himself, to care for his brothers still in this world. Is there opportunity for conversion after bodily death? Does the love of God at last bridge the great gulf? We dare not ask: we may only hope.

Lord of love, who carest for the poor and the outcast, arouse in me the spirit of compassion, lead me on to show my faith through works of mercy, lift me in thought and deed towards the kingdom of heaven where the angels continually praise thy glory.

[Jo, the little crossing-sweeper, is dying of deprivation and neglect. A kindly doctor is with him at the end.]

'Jo, my poor fellow!'
  'I hear you, sir, in the dark, but I'm a gropin – a gropin – let me catch hold of your hand.'
  'Jo, can you say what I say?'
  'I'll say anythink as you say, sir, for I knows it's good.'
  'Our Father'
  'Our Father! – yes, that's wery good, sir.'
  'Which art in Heaven.'
  'Art in Heaven – is the light a comin, sir?'
  'It is close at hand. Hallowed be Thy name!'
  'Hallowed be – thy –'

The light is come upon the dark benighted way. Dead? Dead, your Majesty. Dead, my lords and gentlemen. Dead, Right Reverends and Wrong Reverends of every order. Dead, men

and women, born with Heavenly compassion in your hearts.
And dying thus around us, every day.

Charles Dickens (1812–1870) *Bleak House*

Second Sunday after Trinity
Luke 14.16–24

This parable has been used for sermons against people not coming
to church. It is easy to find modern parallels for the excuses: 'I've
just moved into a new house and I am working on it'; 'I have bought
a new car and want to give it a long drive'; 'I have a lot of family
affairs to attend to.' The problem is of course that these exhortations
are being directed at people who can hear them because they have
already come to church. When Jesus spoke these words he would
have been giving a warning to those who would not respond to the .
good news of the salvation which was being offered. When his own
people rejected him, he turned to the Gentiles and the apostles were
sent out beyond Judea and Samaria to preach to strangers in distant
lands. The lasting message is that God desires all people to be gathered into the kingdom of his love; as in other parables Jesus spoke of
the great final harvest, and the gathering of sheep into one fold. The
Church of God now encompasses the whole world, but the reign of
our Lord is not complete. We may not all be called to be missionaries in the traditional sense, but we are called to spread the faith as
we may, perhaps to confront people tactfully and lovingly about the
opportunity which is set before them. But it is all too easy to live as
if promises and exhortations were directed only at other people. We
may be coming to church regularly, but are we always well prepared
for worship? Do we stay away from the Lord's Table or approach
it without deep reverence? For centuries after the Reformation the
full Communion service was neglected in our Church, and people
received the sacrament infrequently. Now it has happily become
central to our worship and is freely and regularly offered. There is
always danger of corruption of that which is good, and it may be
that we take this great central act of worship for granted and do

not honour it as we should. The feast is prepared but our response may not always be gracious. When his chosen guests failed to come, the rich host invited, and then even constrained, those who were in real need, the disadvantaged and outcasts of society. Now in our time, these are laid to our charge, for material succour as we may be able to provide it, and for the spiritual comfort which they may never have known. God calls those who seem far from him and his infinite love draws them in. Sometimes he is calling upon us to play our part in leading others to the great feast.

Almighty Father, who dost call the people of this world to know thy love and accept thy gift of salvation, may thy light shine upon the suffering and unfortunate among us, and make me a channel of hope for those whose lives touch mine.

Love bade me welcome: yet my soul drew back,
    Guilty of dust and sin.
But quick-eyed Love, observing me grow slack
    From my first entrance in,
Drew nearer to me, sweetly questioning,
    If I lacked any thing.

'A guest', I answered, 'worthy to be here':
    Love said, 'You shall be he'.
'I, the unkind, the ungrateful? Ah my dear,
    I cannot look on thee'.
Love took my hand, and smiling did reply,
    'Who made the eyes but I?'

'Truth, Lord, but I have marred them: let my shame
    Go where it doth deserve'.
'And know you not', says Love, 'who bore the blame?'
    My dear, then I will serve.'
'You must sit down', says Love, 'and taste my meat'.
    So I did sit and eat.

George Herbert (1593–1633) 'Love', *Works*

Third Sunday after Trinity
Luke 15.1–10

This passage begins with one of what are sometimes called the 'conflict stories' in the Gospels, occasions when the growing antagonism to Jesus of the Jewish religious authorities was made clear. Pride, bigotry, failure to understand the new message of love, were gradually opening the road to Calvary. He is attracting to himself those considered to be outside proper obedience to the Law, including publicans – the tax-gatherers who served the Roman power and made dishonest exactions. They found acceptance and welcome in this new Teacher; one of them, Matthew, became one of the Twelve. Jesus answers his opponents with two short and homely analogies. His image as Good Shepherd has already been shown, but now it goes beyond protection of the flock and ensuring that all are safely in the fold. This is the shepherd who goes out to seek one sheep that has gone astray, searching with personal discomfort and possible danger, tenderly carrying the weary one back to safety. This is the shepherd who will not seek his ease while any of his sheep are lost. This is the shepherd who in time will lay down his life for the sheep. We may think of sheep as simple and innocent, but they are also rather stupid creatures, needing to be watched, and liable to wander off on their own affairs. We are more like sheep in their waywardness than in their innocence, and can well take to ourselves the text 'All we like sheep have gone astray' (Isaiah 53.6). The search for the lost coin is very striking – the lighting of a candle, feeble but the only light available, the sweeping through the house until the coin is found, the rejoicing that lost money has been restored to the woman, a poor household where even a slight loss could bring deprivation or disaster. Both in the world of work and in domestic life, things which may seem trivial can be deeply valued. The searches described in these parables present God's deep desire for us; for our spiritual health more precious to him than a sheep even to a most loving shepherd. Both stories end with the comment that repentance of sin brings joy not only on earth but even in heaven. Our short and often grubby little lives have meaning within the great cosmos of God's creation. With little knowledge of sheep, and with coins becoming less common than paper or electronic transactions, we still hear the call to repent, to accept the love of the great friend of sinners. If he rejoices when we turn back to him, how warmly should we respond to the signs of grace in other people, to welcome without reserve those whom the world may despise.

Most loving God, whose desire is always that sinners will repent and return to thee, give me true contrition and longing for amendment of life, restore in me the wholeness which sin has broken, shield me from the temptations which will in the future beset me.

O Shepherd with the bleeding feet,
   Good Shepherd with the pleading voice,
      What seekest Thou from hill to hill?
Sweet were the valley pastures, sweet
   The sound of flocks that bleat their joys,
      And eat and drink at will.
Is one worth seeking, when Thou hast of Thine
      Ninety and nine?

How should I stay My bleeding feet,
   How should I hush My pleading voice?
      I who chose death and climbed a hill,
Accounting gall and wormwood sweet,
   That hundredfold might bud My joys
      For love's sake and good will.
I seek My one, for all there bide of Mine
      Ninety and nine.

Christina Rossetti (1830–1894) 'O, Shepherd with the bleeding feet', *Poems*

Fourth Sunday after Trinity
Luke 6.36–42

These are words of clear ethical teaching. Some people like to
think of Jesus as simply a great ethical teacher and believe that to
follow his precepts is enough to claim to be a Christian. But the
rule of life which he taught is to be obeyed because it comes from
the will of God and is directed towards our part in showing to the
world the love which he continually pours into it. Here we are told
that we must show mercy to others because God is merciful to us.
In the words of Portia in Shakespeare's *The Merchant of Venice*,
mercy 'is an attribute of God himself'. The images that Jesus uses
are, as always, not remote but such as can be understood through
familiar everyday living: the measuring out of corn, the predica-
ment of one blind man leading another, dealing with foreign
bodies in the eye. The last example has the exaggerated humour
which Jesus, like the Rabbis of his time and later, sometimes used
to emphasize a point. Self-righteous censure of others may be like
pointing out a speck of dust in another person's eye with a large
plank of wood sticking out of one's own. We are all in need of
God's mercy. We shall be measured by our own standards, not by
a vengeful God but by the creator of an ordered world in which
deeds and choices have their consequences. Let us then seek to
be cleansed in our own situation, by repentance, confession and
amendment of life. Let us be on our guard against being judge-
mental in words and attitudes towards others. It is difficult, but
vitally important, to remain true to what we believe, to declare it
as the occasion offers, but at the same time not to condemn those
whose ways and ideas are different from ours. God calls us to be
his missionaries, but not to be his prosecuting counsels. Follow
Jesus, who taught how life should be lived, but forgave those who
opposed and destroyed him, even at the last pleading for those
who were nailing him to the cross. To forgive enemies, not to
use power for the hurt of others, may be the ideal of many who
profess no religious faith. Christians know that they can hope to
achieve the ideal only through strength given by God, who shows
mercy when we deserve judgement. Jesus reveals God in humanity,

teaching that the ideal is not imposed by a distant tyrant but is in fact a share in the divine nature. We are being allowed to do the things that God does, to feel the compassion that he feels. A few minutes thinking about what we really deserve, and the mercy which has so often spared us from the consequences of sin and folly, should bring us to a better understanding of the commandments of love. Our own imperfection may be as obvious to others, and certainly is to God, as that awkward plank of wood.

Almighty God, who dost continually pardon the sins of those who repent, and hast given us in thy son the pattern of perfection, grant me a clear vision of my own sins, humble love towards the faults of others and grace to grow nearer every day to my Lord and Saviour.

The essence of all purification is self-simplification; the doing away of the unnecessary and unreal, the tangles and complications of consciousness: and we must remember that when these masters of the spiritual life speak of purity, they have in their minds no thin, abstract notion of a rule of conduct stripped of all colour and compounded chiefly of refusals, such as a more modern, more arid asceticism set up. Their purity is an affirmative state; something strong, clean, and crystalline, capable of a wholeness of adjustment to the wholeness of a God-inhabited world. The pure soul is like a lens from which all irrelevancies and excrescences, all the beams and motes of egotism and prejudice, have been removed; so that it may reflect a clear image of the one Transcendent Fact within which all other facts are held.

Evelyn Underhill (1875–1941) *Practical Mysticism*

Fifth Sunday after Trinity
Luke 5.1–11

This is a detailed and dramatic episode early in our Lord's ministry. It may seem remote to a modern reader, not familiar with fishing by nets from small boats on a lake, but it relates to the experience of many believers, culminating in a promise and a challenge. The men were weary and discouraged after a toilsome night which had produced nothing. The last thing they, or we, would want when things have gone wrong is to be told to go back and try the same thing again. But the words came with authority, and with command for even greater effort – 'launch out into the deep'. This was One who had to be obeyed, and the tired fishermen rowed out again. The result was overwhelming, the bounty so great that it aroused fear rather than joy and even seemed to threaten their safety. Peter, impetuous as he always was, could not bear it and begged to be left alone for a quiet life. But his new friend comforted him, and called him to greater things, to a life of service in telling the good news of salvation. It is an experience not confined to the Galilean lake. Disappointment, awareness of a divine word, reluctant obedience, the inescapable power of abundant grace, reassurance, direction towards a new way of service; this in many ways has been the experience of Christians. Silently, secretly, but irresistibly, any of us may be called to launch out into the deep. Go right out, not near the shore where the return will be easy if nothing happens, but far into the deep water. There was the place of disappointment where nothing was found. There now is the place of success, so great that it is overwhelming, brings new peril, new fear, and a new command. There is the revelation that the voice that commands is the voice of God. Many, perhaps most, of those who have been clearly called to serve God in a particular way have reacted at first with alarm and disbelief. All who claim to trust in him must be ready to respond if the call comes to them.

O God who hast called thy people to follow in the way of service and obedience, give me courage to overcome fear and disappointment, and to know, accept and obey thy will for me now and all through my life.

True faith is confident, and will venture all the world upon the strength of its persuasion. Will you lay your life on it, your estate and your reputation, that the doctrine of Jesus Christ is true in every article? Then you have true faith. But he that fears men more than God, believes men more than he believes in God. Faith, if it be true, living, and justifying, cannot be separated from the good life; it works miracles, makes a drunkard become sober, a lascivious person become chaste, a covetous man become liberal; 'it overcomes the world – it works righteousness', and makes us diligently to do, and cheerfully to suffer, whatsoever God hath placed in our way to heaven.

Jeremy Taylor (1613–1667) *The Rule and Exercises of Holy Living*

Sixth Sunday after Trinity
Matthew 5.20–26

This is part of the long discourse commonly known as the Sermon on the Mount. Many people imagine it as a sort of public address by Jesus speaking from the top of a mountain to a crowd below. The point is that the sight of the 'multitude' moved him to withdraw to a mountain-top where he spoke to his closest followers – 'disciples' here probably meaning more than the Twelve. He censures the Scribes and Pharisees, representatives of the most severe religious people, not for their observance and teaching of the Jewish Law but for their narrow interpretation of its precise letter. It was this kind of open criticism which brought him increasingly into conflict with the religious establishment and eventually to their engineering his judgement and death. Jesus gives this warning as part of a deeper understanding of the commandment not to commit murder. To come closer to the whole problem of violence, abuse and bitterness is challenging. Look down the long road that begins with a burst of impatience and ends with the killing of another human being. There are many stages on it – how far has any one of us reached? How confident is any one of us that the road does not suddenly drop into a steep slope that carries the traveller inescapably along to the end? 'Be careful,' says Jesus, 'you who rely on the letter of a law that you have no temptation to break. My new law of love makes you free from legalistic fear, but it lays a new obligation on you, a true gentleness that does not hide behind pious words.' The commandments of God remain strong and binding, for they require not formal obedience to rules but the harder way of self-denial and love. We must grow up and leave our natural inclinations behind so that we may be faithful in his service.

We are disciples, coming close to Jesus, listening to his teaching about how life should be lived by those who claim to follow him. The danger of formal religion, outward conformity becoming a block to the inner spirit, has not gone away. Religious duties and formal worship are part of Christian obedience, but they are not enough in themselves. Few indeed will commit murder, or come close to it – even if we sometimes say things like, 'I could murder him for it.' But words spoken with exasperation can come from hidden anger, the beginning of a perilous path that can lead to worse things. Insults, spoken or thought, are part of the same danger. The word *'Raca'* suggests emptiness or worthlessness, and it is indeed a terrible thing to regard as worthless any human creature for whom Jesus Christ died. Going to church with bitter feelings, with contempt for anyone, makes a mockery of worship. John reminds us that it is not possible truly to love God if we do not love other people (1 John 4.20). 'Reconciliation' is a fine word, whether it is used of two individuals or on an international scale. It is the image of the Christian, the fulfilment of the words of Jesus in this same discourse, 'blessed are the peacemakers'. In our self-examination, sins of word and thought are as important to acknowledge as sins of action.

Heavenly Father, whose love for this sinful world was revealed through the suffering and death of thy dear Son, raise up in me the love which so often fails, and strengthen me to show that love through the spirit of peace and reconciliation which comes by thy grace alone.

These words of our Lord are a challenge, an impeachment and an indictment of high treason against those in authority in the Church. No man who uttered such words, under such conditions, could escape retaliation. Had our Lord contented Himself with His wonderful works, He might have walked across Calvary unscathed. But one who could say such things as this, under such circumstances, must come to the cross. Those who are so challenged were certain to encompass His death. For I want you just to notice who the challenge was made against. It was made against the great religious teachers of the day, the Scribes and Pharisees. They were the oracles of the kingdom, and in no case could they enter into the kingdom whose oracles they held. They stood with the keys of the door that all others might go in, but they themselves could not go in. 'In no case shall ye enter into the kingdom of heaven.' You know how the case stood, how religion had become formal, mechanical. You cannot turn out righteousness from any machine. Directly religion becomes a system, it loses its power. Systematised religion degenerates always, sooner or later, into formalism. It was so then, and has been ever since.

A. H. Stanton (1839–1913) *Faithful Stewardship*

Seventh Sunday after Trinity
Mark 8.1–9

We have already met the story of the miraculous feeding as told in John's Gospel, on the Fourth Sunday in Lent. Mark (and also Matthew) give two accounts, with differences in the numbers of the crowd, the loaves and fishes, and the collected remains. It is possible that there were two such events, though the bewilderment of the disciples on the second occasion is hard to understand if they had already witnessed a similar transformation. It is likely that, the miracle being so important as a prefiguring of the Eucharist, more than one memory was being recalled and became recorded. All the Gospel records contain the same essentials: the large crowd, the disciples' worry, the fourfold action, multiplying a small offering, and the fact that there was enough and to spare. Variations in numbers are frequent in the Gospels, and in all early records depending in the first instance on oral transmission. We need seek no fanciful or symbolic interpretations, but can note that in this account it is the compassion of Jesus for the hungry crowd that motivates the action. In John's version, named disciples take part in the initial discussion about what to do. As Mark tells it, Jesus gives the direct command and does not test their knowledge of the situation. In both, the disciples are anxious and helpless. In the words of Mark, who is often quite hard on the Twelve, they do not try to find out what little may be on offer, or even to calculate the cost of feeding all these people. There is a thought for us here. God graciously allows us to join in his works of mercy and the spreading of the good news. Sometimes we seem to have clear instructions: the way is open, the opportunity is here for us to offer our tiny resources. At other times, we find ourselves in an unexpected situation where we can be used. With prayer for further guidance, we are shown what is to be done. Sometimes we need to be taught how to be more open to God's will. Sometimes perhaps it is like a little child 'helping' in the house. God is not depending on us for help and, as with a child, the job may take longer. But God our loving Father surely rejoices to see his children learning and responding. At Holy Communion, the offerings of bread and wine are tiny yet we who receive them are filled with a strength that is not our own. We often also feel physical renewal, emotional calm, a general sense of healing. The miracle in the wilderness is repeated in a more wonderful way. At every moment of the day, the Eucharist is being celebrated somewhere in the world. As the early Church found deeper revelation in the story, our sense of wonder every time we come to receive the sacrament can never be too great.

O God by whom the souls of thy people are nourished by spiritual food, as the bodies of the multitude were wonderfully fed, I give thanks for thy continual bounty and pray that I may faithfully respond when I am called to any service in thy name.

Why should I call Thee Lord, Who art my God?
Why should I call Thee Friend, Who art my Love?
Or King, Who art my very Spouse above?

Or call Thy sceptre on my heart Thy rod?
Lo now Thy banner over me is love,
All heaven flies open to me at Thy nod:
For Thou hast lit Thy flame in me a clod,
Made me a nest for dwelling of Thy Dove.
What wilt Thou call me in our home above?
Who now hast called me friend? How will it be?
When Thou for good wine settest forth the best?
Now Thou dost bid me come and sup with Thee,
Now Thou dost make me lean upon Thy breast:
How will it be with me in time of love?

Christina Rossetti (1830–1894) 'After Communion', *Poems*

Eighth Sunday after Trinity
Matthew 7.15–21

Jesus here gives his teaching through two images which are often found in both Testaments and were well understood by hearers whose life was predominantly pastoral and agricultural. We have already studied his words about sheep and shepherds, the pattern of vulnerability on one side and selfless love on the other. But evil forces can make use of the common belief that sheep are harmless, perhaps a bit stupid but incapable of being a threat. The ravening wolf can get into the fold, even into the home, by putting on a temporary disguise. The image of the wolf in sheep's clothing is proverbial, and expresses the truth that apparent innocence can conceal evil that wicked designs can present themselves as good intentions. Hypocrisy is a sin most often recognized and condemned by Jesus, particularly when it was seen among those who professed special piety and regard for the Law. The idea of getting grapes from thorns or figs from thistles is exaggerated humour to force attention, like the picture of the mote and the beam. The healthy and the rotten tree are still familiar in orchards and gardens. We do not need to be expert fruit-growers to know about natural diseases and rotting fruit. The message is clear.

Good works are not the means of salvation – that comes through the sacrificial love of God. But the failure to seek to live by the will of God displays failure to embrace that salvation sincerely. Obedience and good works are the proof, the good fruit, the sign of spiritual health, of gratitude for the gifts of grace which we do not deserve. There is continually a temptation to be satisfied with a profession of faith, claims to be a Christian, attending public worship. These are right and necessary but they are not enough. Formal prayer, public or private, can become empty, a form of words, a task to be accomplished. We all suffer from distractions, disinclination to pray. There are times when we would rather not open ourselves to God in prayer, perhaps uncomfortably aware that our inner selves are already open to him and it is response, not initiative, which is required. There are times when we feel it is an effort to go to church. God is merciful, accepting and sanctifying what we offer if the deeper desire is genuine: the imperfect act of will is lifted into an act of faith. The wolves are all around us, some exploiting good causes and human needs for what they can get. It is not only the great deceits, the notorious dishonesty, that threaten us. Temptations come in many ways, often under attractive disguises and even apparently holy cover. The Christian is never more at risk than when feeling assured of being in a state of grace and needing no divine support. We need to recognize these temptations, and also to recognize the wolf within ourselves. Weakness is forgiven; deliberate disobedience and misuse of privilege is spiritual death, like the end of the diseased tree. Submission to the law of love will keep the wolf from our door.

Lord God, Maker and Judge of all, from whose grace alone all good works proceed, give me sincere faith, willing obedience, and a way of life following the steps of Christ my Saviour.

Now the wolf is the devil, he lieth in wait to deceive, and they that follow him; for it is said that 'they are clothed indeed with the skins of sheep, but inwardly they are ravening wolves'. If the hireling observe anyone indulging in wicked talking, or in sentiments to the deadly hurt of his soul, or doing ought that is abominable and unclean, and notwithstanding that he seems to bear a character of some importance in the Church (from which if he hopes for advantage he is an hireling) says nothing.

Augustine (354–430) *On Matthew 7.15*

Ninth Sunday after Trinity
Luke 16.1–9

This is one of the Bible passages that preachers would rather avoid as matter for a sermon. Known as the Parable of the Unjust Steward, it is difficult to interpret. It may have been a warning to those who were prosperous and influential but would eventually lose their power and need to find support where they could. But the words are addressed to the disciples, and this is a difficulty. The tone is ironical, spoken with what we may venture to call the dry humour Jesus often brought into his teaching. It is unfortunate that the Prayer Book reading omits the verses immediately following, which have the clear message that if we are not honest and faithful in small matters, we shall not respond worthily to the greater blessings and responsibilities which God will bestow upon us. 'Mammon' means material wealth and we are warned that 'Ye cannot serve God and Mammon' (verse 13). If we read and reflect on these words, the oddness of the parable is not completely solved, but a new meaning emerges from it. Dishonesty with money, or in anything where people trust us, is not excusable because amounts are small, or if our concessions seem to be benefiting someone else, as well as being to our own advantage. We are too familiar with dishonesty and breach of trust in our society today, bringing temptation to people who have positions of respect and authority, and sometimes causing their downfall. Let us not be complacent because we have not the scope for spectacular faults. Let us not ignore the smaller temptations. Just as spiritual progress is made slowly, with little steps and a continual desire to come closer to true obedience, so there can be little steps downward, each one making it easier to break faith in something more. Life does not stand still and we may come to the end of each day a little nearer in our response to faith, or having drifted a little further away. St Thérèse of Lisieux wrote of the 'little way' which makes spiritual progress in small steps. Unhappily, the negative way can be equally real, perhaps easier to follow in our liability to sin, until what had seemed harmless and negligible becomes serious, offering the next backward step. There is always a danger of 'scruples', of being so concerned with every detail that the liberty of God's love is forgotten, but there is a greater danger of becoming more and more unscrupulous in the popular sense. A good citizen of heaven will not be a bad citizen of earth.

Almighty God, by whose love created the world and all that is therein, have mercy on our misuse of what is entrusted to us. Keep me in the way of honest living and give me grace to resist the temptation of material gain wrongly acquired.

As money creates money, as the land bears bread, wine, and oil, so our souls should yield the due return to God for the many gifts which He has bestowed upon us. All these are God's gifts to us, and they are given us, not to be wasted, but to be used, to be turned to account. The Steward in the parable wasted them, and was made responsible for his waste. And so in our own case, we may waste them, as most men waste them; nay, worse, we may not only squander them away, we do not know how; but we may actually misapply them, we may use them actually to the injury of Him who has given them to us; but whether we do nothing with them for God, or actually go on to use them to His dishonour and against the interests of truth and religion (and the latter is more likely than the former, for not to do good with them is in fact to do evil), anyhow we shall have one day to answer for our use of them. Thus the parable before us applies to all of us, as having certain goods committed to us by our Divine Master with a day of reckoning for them in prospect. But this is not all. Charges were brought against the Steward, and his employer called on him to answer them, or rather examined them, and found them well founded. And so it is sometimes with us, that our conscience, which is the voice of God in the soul, upbraids us, brings before us our neglect of duty, the careless, the irreligious, the evil life which we are leading, our disregard of God's commands, glory and worship.

J. H. Newman (1801–1890) *Parochial and Plain Sermons*

Tenth Sunday after Trinity
Luke 19.41–47

The shortest verse in the Bible consists of the two words 'Jesus wept', telling of his response to the death of Lazarus and the mourning of the bereaved family and friends. Later, he wept for the collective sorrow that would befall many people. Luke records this deep grief as being expressed on Palm Sunday. At the time of his triumphal entry into Jerusalem, Jesus wept for the city and its people, ignorant of what would come upon them within a generation. In AD 70 Jerusalem was besieged by the Romans, entered and destroyed, its people scattered. The perfect humanity of Jesus is shown in this outward sign of pity, the bodily response to deep inner feeling. The people had greeted him with enthusiasm, with shouts of 'Hosanna' – 'Save now', but after a few days they would see their King condemned and crucified. Not many years later, their children and their children's children would lose their holy city and all that it stood for. Divinity knew what was to come, humanity saw people living in a world of uncertainty and suffering: both responses of suffering love were united in the incarnate Christ. It was a day of apparent triumph and a day of infinite pity. It was also a day of judgement. The Temple, once destroyed, rebuilt with resolve and faith, the centre of worship, was profaned by its commercial use, taking advantage of citizens and strangers who came to make their offerings. The sorrow of Jesus turned to righteous anger and stern action. The Temple, built to the honour of God, designed for his continual worship, was being used as a source of gain. It too would perish, destroyed even to the ground when Jerusalem fell. The Bible tells of the love of God. It tells also of his holiness and his anger. Mercy always follows repentance. But deliberate defiance falls under judgement. We still fail in reverence, personal and collective, towards our consecrated places of worship. We still sometimes value the material above the spiritual. We still pay lip-service to the holiness revealed in Jesus Christ but do not honour him in our lives and make the good news of his redemption known to others. After the stirring events of the day, in the short time left before his Passion, Jesus taught in the Temple. With dreadful suffering to come, he desired only that his people should know and obey the will of God. Through all the years, his word continues for those who will hear it, his teaching remains true after many human calamities, sanctified and proved by his own sacrificial death on the cross.

Lord of all mercy, who dost regard with sorrow our failures to understand thy purpose, forgive my ignorance and indifference, fill me with reverence for thy holiness, and open my ears to the unending message of thy love.

Why doth my Saviour weep
 At sight of Sion's bowers?
Shows it not fair from yonder steep,
 Her gorgeous crown of towers?
Mark well His holy pains:
 'Tis not in pride or scorn,
That Israel's King with sorrow stains
 His own triumphal morn.

It is not that His soul
 Is wandering sadly on,
In thought how soon at death's dark goal
 Their course will all be run,
Who now are shouting round
 Hosanna to their chief;
No thought like this in Him is found,
 This were a Conqueror's grief

Or doth He feel the Cross
    Already in His heart,
The pain, the shame, the scorn, the loss?
    Feel e'en His God depart?
No: though He knew full well
    The grief that then shall be –
The grief that angels cannot tell –
    Our God in agony.

It is not thus He mourns;
    Such might be martyr's tears,
When his last lingering look he turns
    On human hopes and fears;
But hero ne'er or saint
    The secret load might know,
With which His Spirit waxeth faint;
    His is a Saviour's woe.

John Keble (1792–1866) 'Tenth Sunday after Trinity'

Eleventh Sunday after Trinity
Luke 18.9–13

This short and simple parable is a warning against the fault which
Jesus often condemned in his teaching. The Pharisees have gained
a bad name in modern usage, made almost equivalent to 'hypo-
crites'. They were the strictest Jews of the time, seeking to obey
every observance of the Mosaic Law and to avoid any contami-
nation either physical or devotional. They are not to be seen as
bad people, but as those whose continual anxiety about religious
matters could sometimes lead to introspection and then to a sense
of being superior to others whose way of life was more casual.
Their belief that keeping the Law made them righteous too often
led to complacency, and then to arrogance about the shortcom-
ings of others. It is not surprising that they clashed with Jesus,
who taught that people must seek for righteousness deep within

themselves. He did not condemn ritual observance, but made it uncomfortably clear that outward conformity was useless if it excluded humility and compassion. Publicans were agents of the system of taxation imposed by the Roman occupying authority, the end of a chain of transactions by which they had the power to collect what was due; they were generally dishonest and extortionate, exacting more than they should, and bitterly disliked by their compatriots. Jesus was more than once blamed for being in their company and sharing meals with them. In this story, the Pharisee praises himself for both negative and positive obedience. He does not commit moral offences, and he obeys the rules of fasting and almsgiving, noting the publican who stands near him as an example to be avoided. His words are supposed to be offered towards God, but in substance they are self-centred and complacent. The publican does not tell God about details, but simply acknowledges his sinful state and his need for mercy. This parable is yet another example of the Gospel reversals of social expectations: the despised tax-gatherer who acknowledges his sin is the one who wins approval. Self-righteousness is a continual temptation in the practice of faith and worship. The message is clear, the warning is sharp. There is no way to true repentance but perfect honesty and true humility. In the words of the psalmist, 'A broken and contrite heart, O God, shalt thou not despise' (Psalm 51.17). The cry of the Christian must always be, 'God be merciful to me a sinner.' The danger in sincerely avoiding spiritual pride is the insidious temptation to be proud in one's humility, to feel good by really wanting not to be bad. There is a story of a Sunday school teacher who, after careful explanation of this parable, said, 'Now, children, let us thank God that we are not like that Pharisee.'

Most loving God, who dost forgive all sins that are truly repented, grant me the spirit of penitence, cleanse me from all pride, delusion and self-satisfaction, be merciful to me, a sinner.

According to scholars, pride is nothing other than love of your own excellence; that is, of your own reputation. Therefore the more you love and delight in your own reputation, the greater is your pride, and the greater is this wicked image within you. If pride stirs in your heart, leading you to imagine yourself holier, wiser, better, and more virtuous than others, or that God has given you grace to serve Him better than others; or if you regard other men and women as inferior to yourself, and hold exaggerated opinions of your own excellence in comparison with others; or if as a result you feel complacent and self-satisfied, it is a sure sign that you bear this black image within you. And although it may be hidden from the eyes of other men, it appears clearly in the sight of God.

Walter Hilton (1340–1396) *The Ladder of Perfection*

Twelfth Sunday after Trinity
Mark 7.31–37

Jesus has come into Gentile territory, beginning the preaching of the kingdom which the apostles will continue in the new Church and which will in time be preached throughout the world. He has healed the daughter of the Canaanite woman and is on the way back to cross the Sea of Galilee and return to his own land. He meets and miraculously heals a man afflicted in both speech and hearing. We can try to imagine the suffering of such a person at a time when there was no means of therapy, and when any kind of disability aroused indifference or even hostility rather than compassion. One word from the Lord is enough to take away the impediment and restore the man to wholeness. We are told the precise word that he used, '*Ephphatha*'. In his Gospel Mark gives a few such examples of the Aramaic language which Jesus spoke and which was the common language of his people at that time. Few today have any knowledge of it, but there is a kind of thrill in knowing exactly what words came from those holy lips, as we realize that what Jesus said has come to us from Aramaic through Greek and into English. What brings us even closer is the detail of the sigh as he looked up to heaven. What was the meaning of that typically human expression of disquiet? Was it the sorrow of

God for human suffering, distress that people came more often for physical than for spiritual healing, or a moment of human weariness at the continual demands on him? Jesus Christ, true God and true man stands there before us. He was performing the works of healing which were to be signs of the Messiah, a witness to those around him and a sign to all ages. Still there is compassion for the suffering of the world, still prayers are too often for selfish ends, still people turn to God when there is trouble and forget him when things are going well. In all languages prayers are made and prayers are heard. If ears are truly open, the word of God comes to direct and to make whole. On this Sunday we often remember people who are suffering from any kind of speech or hearing disability, and pray for them and for those who can help them. There is also a message here for all of us, blessed as most of us are with the normal use of our faculties. We should pray constantly that our ears may be open to hear the word of God, not shutting it out through indifference, inattention or overfamiliarity. We should also pray for grace and opportunity to speak the words of salvation that we have received, making known the great things which God has done for us. Speech and hearing, like all his gifts, are to be used in his service, and we pray that they may indeed be open. After his miracles of healing, Jesus sometimes told the one who was cured to make known what God had done for him; sometimes, as on this occasion, he enjoined silence. The gratitude of the healed man and his friends felt no restraint and they made it known. His growing fame as a healer was one of the things that made his enemies work against him. We who know the whole story, and worship him in his divinity, can freely speak his praise.

Lord whose healing power goes out into all the world, have mercy on those who suffer defects of speech or hearing and give them release. Open my ears to hear thy word, loosen my tongue to tell thy goodness, make me a channel of thy love.

As Thou hast touch'd our ears, and taught
    Our tongues to speak Thy praises plain,

Quell Thou each thankless godless thought
 That would make fast our bonds again.
From worldly strife, from mirth unblest,
Drowning Thy music in the breast,
From foul reproach, from thrilling fears,
Preserve, good Lord, Thy servants' ears.

From idle words, that restless throng
 And haunt our hearts when we would pray,
From Pride's false chime, and jarring wrong,
 Seal Thou my lips, and guard the way:
For Thou hast sworn, that every ear,
Willing or loth, Thy trump shall hear,
And every tongue unchained be
To own no hope, no God, but Thee.

John Keble (1792–1866) 'Twelfth Sunday after Trinity'

Thirteenth Sunday after Trinity
Luke 10.23–37

While such parables as the Unjust Steward present a problem for preachers, this story is so well known that it challenges them to say something new. But the message of neighbourly love is so important that there is no need to seek for novelty. The central figure is a Samaritan, a man from the territory north of Judea and Galilee, where the population were descendants of Jews from the old northern kingdom, mixed with those from other lands introduced there after its fall. They were despised by the Jews of the south, regarded as imperfect in their faith and corrupt in their worship. Jesus more than once treated them with courtesy, both in practice and in story. The Samaritan is the only one of the passers-by to care for the wounded traveller. He is not called 'good': the phrase 'The Good Samaritan' comes from a page-heading in the King James Version. His reaction is simply narrated without comment. The word here rendered as 'compassion' is very strong in the Greek, suggesting a disturbance in one's inward parts; elsewhere it is used of Jesus himself. To say, 'It really turned him over inside' would come nearer to it. Not by the command of the Law, not by social conscience, but by feeling for another human being in distress. No matter for the hostility between Jews and Samaritans, the religious disputes, the avoidance of personal relationships. This was the neighbour, the one who was near and needed help. Seeing was followed by action, emergency treatment, money given for further care. Those who came first to the scene of the robbery did not fail to notice the victim; they were so strongly aware of him that they kept their distance to avoid being made virtually unclean by contact with him. They did not remember that the duty to love one's neighbour as oneself was contained in the Law that they professed to follow. The lawyer who asks the question which is answered by a story was a professional interpreter of the Law, claiming authority in matters of its application. He is surprised by the answer that Jesus gives, but has the honesty to accept its implication. The parable leaves us with a command to be compassionate, not merely noticing or even being sympathetic, but truly caring for the suffering to others. Love for God is totally joined with love for his people. All races and societies are objects of his love, and it is a sin for us to regard any of them as inferior or less worthy of respect. The commandments of God may sometimes seem intimidating and calling for heroic efforts. The opportunity for obedience often lies nearer than we think, and if we aspire too far into the distance we may miss what lies immediately before us. There is also another thought: do not casually enquire into the mysteries of faith, unless you are prepared for an unexpected and challenging answer.

Heavenly Father, whose law is the law of love, break through the sins of prejudice and selfishness, and give to thy people true compassion. Forgive my many failures to love my neighbour, and lead me into the path of righteousness for thy name's sake.

To Mercy, Pity, Peace, and Love
All pray in their distress;
And to these virtues of delight,
Return their thankfulness.

For Mercy, Pity, Peace, and Love
Is God, our Father dear,
And Mercy, Pity, Peace, and Love
Is man, his child and care.

For Mercy has a human heart,
Pity a human face,
And Love, the human form divine,
And Peace, the human dress.

William Blake (1756–1827) 'The Divine Image', *Songs of Innocence*

Fourteenth Sunday after Trinity
Luke 17.11–19

'Leprosy' is a word which still has frightening connotations, even though it has largely, but not entirely, disappeared from the world. In the Bible the leper is a person to be shunned from society, excluded from religious privileges and regarded with horror. There was no cure for this terrible disease which carried a moral stigma as well as causing bodily damage and disfigurement. Until well into the Christian era, the leper was similarly regarded, though religious orders sometimes established leper-houses to isolate and care for sufferers. We can have some idea of the sad situation when we read of this little group wandering together outside the villages in the lonely places of north Judea. A Samaritan was accepted among the Jewish outcasts, a man from the region that was despised by the orthodox. The men stood well away from the healthy ones, as they were required to do, and called out in their misery. They hoped that Jesus could help them, and in faith they believed his word and accepted his command, which was to do what the Law required and prove before a priest that they were cured. But it was only the 'stranger', the outsider, who did not complete his journey until he had turned back and given thanks to his healer. Once again, as in action and in story, Jesus finds the true response of faith in one considered outside the Law. Like the Roman centurion who felt unworthy to have Jesus in his house, the Canaanite woman who pleaded for her daughter, here was one who recognized the divine presence and by his response put to shame many who professed to keep the Law. The Holy Spirit comes as a particular gift of power to the Church, but it is a great mistake to think that power to be limited to the Church. The grace of God touches many who do not regard themselves as religious, who may express various shades of indifference and even actual unbelief. Perhaps they feel inside themselves the need of someone to thank for the gifts that have no human giver, and the way is opened for an act of faith that may not even be realized in this world. Praise to God for it, and also possibly an uncomfortable feeling about the depth of our gratitude to the God whom we claim to worship through his Son.

This story gives an example which is continually needed. We are to render thanks to God at all times, and particularly when he relieves our distress and anxiety. How often do we ask for some benefit, and fail to give special thanks when it is granted? Let us remember also that although 'leper' has almost ceased to be a literal description, there is still stigma attached to other illnesses. It is only slowly that there is compassion for those affected by the HIV/AIDS epidemic. Mental health conditions often arouse suspicion and hostility. We have a long way to go on the road of compassion. There is one more thought. The lepers were cleansed 'as they went', while they were walking towards Jerusalem. It is as we go about our daily lives, and not only in times of personal or public worship, that our souls will be healed.

Send thy blessing, O Lord of love, upon all who are shunned or feared for any infirmity of mind or body. Give to us all the love which casts out fear and seeks the good of others. Make me ever thankful for all thy mercies, and walk beside me day by day.

All that is required of the most perfect Christian may be contained in this 'giving him thanks'; giving thanks, always in word and deed, to Christ, for His great deliverance and salvation.

Is he compassionate and merciful, active in giving of alms, fervent in prayer, careful in practices of mortification and self-denial; does he labour to offer up his whole body as a living sacrifice to God, acceptable through Jesus Christ? All this is nothing else but a giving of thanks for his salvation. And therefore it is that love, joy, and peace are inseparable from every duty of a Christian, because his heart is the seat of thanksgiving. What more natural? What more easy? How much more so is this conduct of the thankful leper, than the miserable pride and forgetfulness of those who went their way and gave no thanks!

Isaac Williams (1802–1865) *Sermons* 1855

Fifteenth Sunday after Trinity
Matthew 6.24–34

We return to the Sermon on the Mount, now to a passage concerned not so much with our conduct as our attitude to life. It is certainly not an encouragement to being irresponsible and failing to organize our lives, but it does condemn the restrictions which we lay on ourselves by continual worry. In a word, we are not to be careless, but to be carefree. We are not to run ahead of God. His time is not our time and his design will be made known when he chooses, not when we think it should be. Worrying about what now seems uncertain is a denial of his loving purpose for all that he has made. God our Father loves the whole of his creation. If he cares for the recurring processes of nature, he cares even more deeply for the human race, created in the divine image and redeemed from sin by the divine sacrifice. Strong in the salvation freely given, not by our own merit, we should have the faith to give our lives into the hands of God. It is easy and plainly true to state, more difficult to fulfil. We are prone to worry, and only prayer can free us from ourselves. In these words, Jesus calls us to find and honour our true values, to refuse the evil and follow the good. As the Israelites were challenged long ago, 'Choose you this day whom ye will serve' (Joshua 24.15). The warning against anxiously seeking material prosperity and putting trust in the things of this world had never been more urgent than at the present time, when gain is the driving force of so many. The priority of choice is to seek the kingdom of God before all else, and to be open to how God will lead each of us individually towards it. If our lives are rightly directed, he has great gifts for us, whether they be manifest in our lives or growing secretly within us. In the words of the psalmist, 'Be still, and know that I am God' (Psalm 46.10). In addition to their moral teaching, these words of Jesus give a beautiful and loving picture of the natural world – the birds, the flowers, even the grass which flourishes for a while, is mown down yet continually renewed. What God loves has been put into our power to protect or to destroy. The Christian faith is not an environmentalist cult, but love and care for the environment should be exercised by those who claim to hold that faith. We have powers to preserve or to destroy which were unknown to those who heard Jesus teach on the mountain. Much has been given to us, and much is demanded.

Father of all, praise be to thee for the love which cares for all that thou hast created. Guide me always to choose the good and refuse the evil, to trust thee day by day, and to set my eternal hope in thee alone.

I come in the little things,
Saith the Lord:
Not borne on morning wings
Of majesty, but I have set My Feet
Amidst the delicate and bladed wheat
That springs triumphant in the furrowed sod.
There do I dwell, in weakness and in power;
Not broken or divided, saith our God!
In your strait garden plot I come to flower:
About your porch My Vine
Meek, fruitful, doth entwine;
Waits, at the threshold, Love's appointed hour.

I come in the little things,
Saith the Lord:
Yea! on the glancing wings
Of eager birds, the softly pattering feet
Of furred and gentle beasts, I come to meet
Your hard and wayward heart.
In brown bright eyes
That peep from out the brake, I stand confest.
On every nest
Where feathery Patience is content to brood
And leaves her pleasure for the high emprize
Of motherhood –
There doth My Godhead rest.

I come in the little things,
Saith the Lord:
My starry wings
I do forsake,
Love's highway of humility to take:
Meekly I fit My stature to your need.
In beggar's part
About your gates I shall not cease to plead
As man, to speak with man –
Till by such art
I shall achieve My Immemorial Plan,
Pass the low lintel of the human heart.

Evelyn Underhill (1875–1941) 'I come in the little things',
Immanence

Sixteenth Sunday after Trinity

Luke 7.11–17

Where was Nain, the place made memorable by this one event?
There is a small village called Nein not far from Nazareth which
is probably the site set down for permanent record in the Gospel.
Jesus was on his way from Capernaum, where he had healed the

centurion's servant. Another person in distress touched his nature of perfect love – again that wonderful word of deep feeling translated as 'compassion'. We can try to relate to the situation of the bereaved mother, devastated by the loss of her son, and left with no worldly support except what other family members were prepared to give her. The life of a widow, then and for centuries later, was one of hardship as well as sorrow. On three occasions Jesus restored life to the newly dead: this young man, Lazarus, and the daughter of Jairus. Unlike some of his secret healings, these were witnessed by a number of people, and at Nain there were 'much people of the city'. As his fame spread, so the conflict with the Jewish authorities became more acute and the plot against him more vicious. He was being hailed as a prophet, as a man specially sent and empowered by God. His full time had not yet come; the reality of his person and mission was revealed gradually, brought to its full revelation on the day of resurrection. The love that would redeem humanity was being shown by degrees. It is easy to say, 'Don't cry. Don't be upset.' Jesus does not just say, 'Weep not', and walk away. He immediately uses his power to take away the sorrow. On every such occasion, his words, whether of encouragement or admonition, are followed by action. Jesus, incarnate God, was experiencing the sorrows of human life. Our God knows all that we can feel, not only by the divine omniscience, but by having been here, walked among his people, shared the tears of their grief. For the Jew and for the pagan philosopher, the idea of divine tears was a blasphemy or a nonsense. People pour out their tears before God, pleading for his comfort, but God Incarnate sheds tears with them. He feels with them, not only with the fatherly love of God but with the brotherly love that itself has known sorrow. We cannot raise the dead; most of us can do little to cure illness or relieve physical suffering. We can all try to follow our words of sympathy by whatever kind of help seems possible. We can confirm our care for the suffering one through intercessory prayer. Those who witnessed the miracle were filled with fear and glorified God. The true fear of God is not fright but reverence; the realization of his mighty power draws us to praise him. Many places far away from Nain have experienced the power and the glory.

Gracious Lord, who hast said 'Blessed are they that mourn, for they shall be comforted', look with mercy on the bereaved and give them strength. Grant me the grace of love for others in need, compassion expressed not in words alone, but in such good works as are prepared within thy will for me.

Who says the widow's heart must break,
The childless-mother sink?
A kinder truer voice I hear,
Which e'en beside that mournful bier
Whence parents' eyes would hopeless shrink,

Bids weep no more – O heart bereft,
How strange, to thee, that sound!
A widow o'er her only son,
Feeling more bitterly alone
For friends that press officious round.

Yet is the voice of comfort heard,
For Christ hath touch'd the bier;
The bearers wait with wondering eye,
The swelling bosom dares not sigh,
But all is still, 'twixt hope and fear.

E'en such an awful soothing calm
We sometimes see alight
On Christian mourners, while they wait
In silence, by some church-yard gate,
Their summons to the holy rite.

And such the tones of love, which break
The stillness of that hour,
Quelling th' embittered spirit's strife –
'The Resurrection and the Life
Am I: believe, and die no more'.

John Keble (1792–1866) 'Burial of the Dead'

Seventeenth Sunday after Trinity
Luke 14.1-11

It is sometimes piously but well said that Jesus is the unseen guest at every meal. The evidence of the Gospels is that his presence, always loving, was not always comfortable for those who sat with him. On this occasion he begins by breaking the strict Law of the Sabbath and then challenges the self-righteous ones to consider what concessions to the rule they would be prepared to make in their own interest. He then rebukes those of the company who were scrambling for the most honourable places. Had he perhaps witnessed the sort of unedifying scene when a guest had been demoted and told to sit somewhere else? He had willingly gone to eat with a leading Pharisee, entering the company of those who were becoming increasingly hostile to him. The significant words, 'They watched him' tell us that this was not a friendly invitation but an occasion to seek further evidence against him. Jesus makes no concessions, shows no fear, does not tone down his teaching, but takes the opportunity to speak of humility to those who were failing to exercise it. As so often in his earthly ministry, he sets the law of love and compassion above the rigid Law of ritual observance. We do not need to be reminded of how people still seek for notice and approval, push themselves forward, look for the priority which may bring some advantage. We see it in rushing for the best seats in travelling – we are probably all guilty here. We see it when there may be a chance of getting into the VIP lounge. We see it as people push others aside in hope of being introduced to some influential person. It is a fault which can be seen sometimes even in our places of worship. The possession of a particular pew week by week may be maintained by hints and implications, if no longer by 'pew-rent'. Do we ever allow our rule of life to become so rigid that we will not break it when there is a call on our compassion? The duty is to keep a balance between proper religious discipline and the relaxation of rules to meet a human need. If we are self-centred and make our own valuation of ourselves, forgetting the duty we owe to God and to his people, we are not following his will. If we regard any as less deserving, less important in any way because of race, class or gender, we are not walking in the steps of Jesus, whose enemies and destroyers were the influential ones, while it was the poor and outcasts who pressed close to hear him. He does not judge what is important by the standards of human judgement. That unseen presence at every meal may be telling us to look more closely at our attitudes and motives. He may be moving us down a little, not perhaps in seating, but in the height of our selfishness. To practise humility in this world is to draw nearer to the kingdom where all are accepted, none given precedence, for God is all in all.

It is the convention that religion and politics should never be discussed at a dinner party, and perhaps that is sound advice for the average social gathering. But when Jesus went out for a meal, his host and fellow-guests did not have an easy time. First he healed a sick man – a passage omitted from this selection of the Gospel – and aroused controversy about breaking the Sabbath. He went on to criticize those who were scrambling for the best seats, warned his host that he should be inviting the outcasts of society instead of his rich friends, and then told a story about people who insulted their host by not responding to his invitation. The point of it all is that those who came to the meal were thinking only of themselves instead of being aware of the needs of others for healing, food or shelter. They were too concerned with their own prestige and privilege, putting themselves at the centre of importance. We sometimes speak of Jesus as the unseen guest at every meal: it is a good thought, but not entirely a comfortable one.

Gracious Lord, pattern of humility and love, pardon my sins of pride and selfishness, give me the desire for true humility, that I may know thy presence in all that I do, and in all whom I meet.

Give me the lowest place; not that I dare
Ask for that lowest place, but Thou hast died
That I might live and share
Thy glory by Thy side.

Give me the lowest place: or if for me
That lowest place too high, make one more low
Where I may sit and see
My God and love Thee so.

Christina Rossetti (1830–1894) 'The Lowest Place', *Poems*

Eighteenth Sunday after Trinity
Matthew 22.34–46

Trick questions come in different forms. The motive may be a harmless joke, or it may be a malicious attempt to lead someone into a trap. The question which the lawyer asked Jesus might have been an innocent opening to a profitable theological discussion, but was in fact part of the plot which the religious powers were developing against him. He had seemed to be questioning some of the details of the Law: could he now be tempted into a flawed answer which would condemn him? His reply was simple, drawn from the Scriptures which his opponents were continually studying (Deuteronomy 6.5 and Leviticus 19.18). Here was the basic message of faith: love towards God and towards the people he had created. All that the sacred books could teach flowed from these two great commandments. Then Jesus asks his interrogators a question: whose son is the long-awaited Messiah? The orthodox answer comes – he will be a descendant of King David. But David, then regarded as the author of the psalms, is recorded as calling the Messiah 'my Lord' (Psalm 110.1). Jesus is gradually revealing his true identity; he is not the son of David, but the Son of God. He has just been dealing with the Sadducees who had tried to support their own disbelief in the resurrection of the dead by asking him a foolish question about the position in heaven of a woman who had married seven husbands. The Pharisees, proud of their learning, thought that they could do better than the silenced Sadducees, but they in turn were silenced, and decided that this man was too dangerous to test with questions. The two great commandments have been repeated through the centuries. As always, the basic word for all God's works is love. He is perfect love, and by his grace alone we can offer something of that love in ourselves. It is good to study the Bible, to try to learn more and apply its words in our lives. But it is dangerous to be too proud, and start asking questions to find out knowledge and teaching which have not been revealed. There are difficult passages – we have already met some of them in the Gospels – but they can too easily be made an excuse for passing over the greater truths. The Bible is a complex book, or rather a collection of books, setting down through human reception and in human language the infinite purposes of God and his mighty work in human history. Through narrative, legend, poetry, doctrine, we are brought as close to precept and practice as we need in this life. There is room for much scholarship, but the basic message is very simple. The Pharisees did not give up their malice against Jesus, but on this occasion they had the sense to know when to stop trying to be too clever.

O God who art the source of all wisdom opening the light of truth to thy faithful people, guide and strengthen me in the way of love, that I may always honour thy majesty, and also may bring blessing to others for thy sake.

One of the crowd went up,
And knelt before the Paten and the Cup,
Received the Lord, returned in peace, and prayed
Close to my side; then in my heart I said:

O Christ, in this man's life –
This stranger who is Thine – in all his strife,
All his felicity, his good and ill,
In the assaulted stronghold of his will,

I do confess Thee here,
Alive within this life; I know Thee near
Within this lonely conscience, closed away
Within this brother's solitary day.

Christ in his unknown heart,
His intellect unknown – this love, this art,
This battle and this peace, this destiny
That I shall never know, look upon me!

Christ in his numbered breath,
Christ in his beating heart and in his death,
Christ in his mystery! From that secret place
And from that separate dwelling, give me grace.

Alice Meynell (1847–1922) 'The unknown God', *Oxford Book of Mystical Verse*

Nineteenth Sunday after Trinity
Matthew 9.1–8

Mark tells this story with much more detail (Mark 2.1–12). In his account, the sick man is carried by four of his friends who, unable to get into the crowded house, climb to the roof, break through its surface, and lower the man on his bed to the feet of Jesus. It is a vivid description which must be the recollection of an eyewitness. Matthew's shorter version has all the same essential elements. The sick man has the blessing of caring friends, in a society that had little concern for physical misfortune. Jesus gives release from sin before release from bodily trouble, and in so doing arouses the anger of the learned and righteous; they rightly know that only God can forgive human sin, but they do not know that the man who says these words is indeed God the Son. With divine wisdom, Jesus knows their hostile response and says in effect, 'Fair enough, but both soul and body can be healed.' He immediately releases the man with a command which must call for an act of faith and is obeyed. The man is able to walk away with restored power, carrying the bed to which he had been confined – probably a light pallet. As always, Jesus shows his power not through causing fear, but by an act of mercy. The 'palsy' which he cured was some kind of paralysis; the English word translates a word several times used in the Bible for muscular dysfunction. While the Scribes, the learned interpreters of the Law, were moved to resentment and growing enmity, the ordinary people who witnessed the miracle responded with wonder and praise. Unlike those who thought they had all the answers, the crowd made the proper response to the sign of divine mercy. Jesus had returned to 'his own city', where he would have been familiar at least by sight to many of the people – something which would have increased the indignation of the Scribes who saw him as an ordinary and unregarded member of the population. Perhaps the friends of the sick man were, on the contrary, encouraged rather than made sceptical by a familiar face. We know no more than is set down, but even in its shorter version, this is a wonderful story of human friendship, divine power and compassion, the response of faith and the danger of self-righteousness. Miracles of healing may not be within our power, but there are many of those disabled who can be helped by a little consideration. We pray to know the compassion which Jesus gave, and to avoid the grudging attitude of those who claim superior wisdom, or are impatient with anyone suffering physical or mental disability.

Merciful Lord, by whose healing power thy love is revealed, give strength and comfort to those who suffer loss of bodily power, and make them whole. Give me grace both to feel compassion for the disabled, and to give them whatever help falls in my way.

The Lord's words are often addressed to the heart and thoughts of those to whom He was speaking; therefore to understand this we must consider, that what lay heavily at this poor man's heart was not so much his bodily affliction as the sense of his sins. He had probably, in the bitterness of his heart, felt that his sickness was well deserved, and only the punishment due to his sins; and his only desire was for his sin to be removed. And that he thus needed encouragement we may conclude from our Lord's tender expression to him, calling him 'Son', or 'child', and bidding him 'be of good cheer' on the subject of his sins.

He was perhaps unable to speak on account of the palsy, but his heart and affliction spoke more than words.

Isaac Williams (1802–1865) *Sermons* 1855

Twentieth Sunday after Trinity
Matthew 22.1–14

This is another parable which has caused difficulty to commentators. It is one of the Parables of the Kingdom through which, as his Passion drew near, Jesus spoke in challenging and sometimes startling terms, reversing normal expectations. This parable is immediately followed in the Gospel by the parable of the Labourers in the Vineyard. The meaning of its first part is not obscure. It is a warning to people who hear the call of God and do not respond, being preoccupied with the routine calls on their lives. It could be a warning particularly to the Jewish people that the revelation which they were refusing would soon be open to the Gentile world. The marriage of the king's son may stand for the Church as the Bride of Christ. But the severe penalty for not having a wedding garment seems strange. How could a man called in from the street find special clothes for the occasion? It has been suggested that the host would provide garments for the occasion and that this man had refused or failed to wear one. Literal interpretations, and over-zealous response to conjectures about the customs of the time, can obscure the real meaning of many of the parables. They are not lessons in social history, not advice about proper dress, but forceful and challenging teaching about the life of faith. They are meant to shake our complacency, to bring us into situations where we can see our own fallibility and all that needs amendment in our duty of prayer and living. We are not meant to think of the practical issue, but of a guest who had accepted the invitation, given without demanding special merit, and had shown disrespect for his gracious host and the couple who were being married. He had come for what he could get, lacking any sense of humble gratitude. There are many who, like the guests first invited, will not listen to the message of salvation. There are many who, professing Christian faith, do not accept the gracious invitation of the Eucharist. There are many more who come without proper preparation, casually and with their minds on things of this world: and is there any one of us who is always guiltless in this way? The careless acceptance of God's grace is perhaps worse than refusal. We stand accused if we do not feel and show deep gratitude for the price of redemption in the suffering and death of the Lord. Not one of us has an immaculate wedding garment. But we can show our faith by thanks for what has been given in costly love.

Most generous God, whose love is unbounded and whose gifts are without measure, give to thy people grateful hearts, filled with praise for thy glory. May I always respond graciously to thy call, and serve thee in reverence and humility.

What is meant by the wedding garment? Surely it must refer to something that renders a man an acceptable guest at a wedding, and the absence of which would render his presence unsuitable at such a place, so that he were better away. The marriage garment is well explained of Christian joy of heart, 'the fruit of the Spirit is joy'; and we may add, delight at the presence of the Bridegroom; for this it is which occasions this gladness of heart.

Isaac Williams (1802–1865) *Sermons* 1855

Twenty-first Sunday after Trinity
John 4.46–54

This story of healing is similar to that which Matthew tells about the healing of a centurion's servant (see Epiphany 3). It is a distance healing, a miraculous cure made without contact with the sick person. The centurion is praised for his faith, shown by a foreigner, a member of the occupying army. The nobleman, a Jew, is challenged more searchingly. Must belief always demand some spectacular sign of God's power, some change in the course of nature? The anxious father responds with a simple, heartfelt plea for healing while there is yet life. He has made an act of faith by coming to seek Jesus: it is clear that he has made a journey far enough for it to be the next day before he returns. The healing love is offered, the promise is accepted in faith, the father goes on his way needing no more reassurance. When his family and household understand how the words of Jesus had immediate effect, they respond with faith. In the Fourth Gospel, the miracles are often presented not only for their evidence of caring love but also as signs of the divine power which is in Jesus. The first sign was a miracle at the wedding feast in Cana, when water was turned into wine – a generous act to save those responsible for the occasion from embarrassment. This second sign is a gift of more lasting effect, working not in a passing situation but in a whole life. Do we seek signs and wonders to confirm our faith day by day? There is no doubt that some remarkable and memorable things happen in response to prayer, but the love of God is constant, given in the little things which we accept as a part of the daily routine, but which are all part of his plan for each of us. The whole question of intercessory prayer is raised by this Gospel reading. We are not trying to soften the heart of an arbitrary tyrant. We are not telling God something that he does not know, or has neglected. We are not suggesting that we are helpers necessary for the fulfilling of his purpose. It is a mystery, but it is a mystery of love, willingness to put ourselves beside the subject of intercession, to be used as human agents in whatever is to follow As we try to formulate our thoughts, perhaps too anxious to find the 'right words', do we always listen for the 'still, small voice' in which God is revealed, rather than in the wind and the fire (1 Kings 19.12)? Are our prayers simple and sincere? There is a place for the formal structure and particular language, but at the point of crisis the nobleman cried out, 'Sir, come down ere my child die.'

Lord, *whose compassion never fails, and whose healing power comes to the sick in body and mind, increase my faith, open my eyes to see thee in all things, and accept prayers that are offered in sincerity and simple trust.*

The nobleman in this case was indeed a noble man. Noble in heart in the presence of Him who knoweth all things. He is the Author and Giver of all life. If there is anything in birth, there is something better in intelligence, and what is best of all is Godliness. This nobleman is prostrate at the Master's feet, making his heart's request: 'Sir, Sir, come down ere my child die', and never was that man more noble. Look into his face as he holds up his hands, the very blood of his heart tingling to the very tips, see the expression in his face – and never was that nobleman a more noble man than then. Brethren, there are some who scorn to ask a favour; the asking a favour is as noble as the granting of one. Some of us can hardly bear to ask a favour; we like to give it, yet our Master Jesus Christ when He reigned from the Tree as King said, 'thirst' and one of the men who was putting Him to death gave Him the sponge, and He accepted it from His executioner.

A. H. Stanton (1839–1913) *Last Sermons in St Alban's, Holborn*

Twenty-second Sunday after Trinity
Matthew 18.21–35

This passage immediately follows teaching which Jesus has been giving to his disciples about the need to forgive and seek reconciliation for offences. Peter, always ready with a question, would like a clear formula, a specific limit to guide him. Jesus responds with another of those parables which make their effect by almost ludicrous exaggeration. The contrast between the small and the large debt is unbelievable; no servant could have such a huge sum of money owing. The words which challenge our imagination do in fact come to the heart of the Christian faith. Our sins are forgiven by the atonement made once for all upon the cross. We no longer strive for salvation by good deeds and legal demands. Our assurance lies in God's promise, and our response of true repentance for our continual falls into actual sin. The lord in the parable was willing to forgo a very large sum of money owing to him, moved by what seemed to be a plea for release and a promise to make good. In his mercy, God took on the pains and limitations of a human life, following the course of his love even to an agonizing death. Every time we say the prayer which our Saviour has taught us, we ask to be forgiven as we forgive others. It is a feeble attempt, but acceptable to God, to show that we have grasped something of the amazing sacrifice on Calvary. Is it always a prayer from the heart? It is not enough to say the words, or to give grudging obedience to the divine command. There is always the danger of unresolved resentment, recollection of a past wrong which is allowed to remain and arouse bitter thoughts. Resentment is a terrible thing; it eats away at the soul, it hinders love for others, it holds us in the dark prison although the door has been open to us. It may not always be possible mentally to forget past wrongs, but the response to Peter's question demands a cleansing of bad emotions. 'Forgive' is an easy word to say, for humorous dismissal of a trivial error, or reconciliation after a serious quarrel. A word that can satisfy the ruffled nerves and keep social life smooth without going very deeply. So it must have been from the beginning of human relationships. As often in the teaching of Jesus, it takes a vivid story to bring home the difference between conventional life and the life of the Christian. The agony of the cross is set against the daily response of men and women to each other. God's response to sin is to suffer and die in the person of the humanity that had so offended. Human response is too often the sulky rebuff, the refused hand, and worst of all the unspoken resentment. It is not the debt that incurs the anger of the Lord: it is the unforgiving choice of satisfaction above compassion, the lasting grudge. An act of will can drive away the demons of resentment. The act of will is enabled by prayerful contemplation of the cross.

Merciful God, who dost forgive the sins of all who truly repent, give me grace both to acknowledge my own sins, and also to forgive any who have offended me. Cleanse me from all that hinders my love for others, free me from resentment, and make me ever thankful for pardon given upon the cross.

The Lord has clearly set forth the condition of such pardon; he has stated it as a law and expressed it as a covenant. We can only expect our sins to be forgiven according to the degree that we ourselves forgive those who sin against us. We are informed categorically that we will not be able to obtain what we ask for in respect of our sins unless we have acted ourselves in the same way to those who have sinned against us. Thus our Lord says in another place in Scripture: 'The measure you deal out will be dealt back to you.' Similarly, the servant who refused to cancel his fellow servant's debt, in spite of having had his own debts cancelled by his master, was thrown into prison. Because he refused to be generous to his fellow servant, he forfeited the indulgence that had been shown to him by his master. These ideas Christ sets forth even more directly and stamps it with his own authority when he says: 'Whenever you stand praying, forgive, if you have anything against anyone; so that your Father in heaven will also forgive you your debts. But if you do not forgive, neither will your Father in heaven forgive you your debts.'

Cyprian of Carthage (?–258) 'On the Lord's Prayer'

Twenty-third Sunday after Trinity
Matthew 22.15–22

The pressure of his opponents on Jesus grows stronger as we move through the Gospel story, and now we find an unexpected league of his enemies. It is not certain who exactly made up this groups of 'Herodians', but they were certainly men who supported the position of Herod as Tetrarch of Galilee, the puppet ruler tolerated by the Romans. The Pharisees were the strictest sect of orthodox Jews, opposed to the foreign occupation and unlikely to associate with any who did not keep their strict rules. Now, anxious about the increasing popularity of Jesus, they are determined to trap him. At first seeming to flatter him for his known integrity, they ask him a trick question – should a faithful Jew pay or refuse the tax imposed from Rome? A positive or negative reply would have given them a lever: to refuse would be sedition, an offence to be brought before the ruling power, but to agree would set many people against Jesus as a supporter of foreign domination. He asks for a coin which would be used to pay the Roman tax: it has the image of Caesar, the foreign oppressor. But he does not fall into the trap. Instead he tells his questioners that both authorities, secular and sacred, have claim on our loyalty. There is lawful power which, however unwelcome, is an inescapable part of an ordered society; here is the power of God, Ruler of all, who is not disobeyed when we obey the laws of the state. The men who thought that they had trapped Jesus were silenced and went away without anything more to say. They were not defeated, for in the next verses we read of the Sadducees trying to catch Jesus with another trick question, and immediately after that the Pharisees are back with a question about the Law (see Trinity 18). The first encounter has left its message that Christians are to be good citizens on earth and also live as citizens of the kingdom of God. What if the ruling power is plainly evil? There are times when the individual conscience leads to defiance, and oppressive regimes have made martyrs and continue to do so. It is well if we can live in harmony with our authorities, but there are times when God must be obeyed above Caesar. When discussion of religion gets too hot to be comfortable, it can be a relief to turn to specific issues. 'I asked God for something and he did not give it to me.' 'Why do people fight each other about religion?' 'What do Christians think about paying taxes which may be used for bad purposes?' A clear answer to every question would be so comforting: perhaps a Bible with an index in which one could look up a specific reference to the problem. But this kind of thing is putting God to the test of human values and limited desires. Evidence for God is not found by looking for one who makes life go exactly the way we want it to. We can come to know him only if we acknowledge him as one whose power is supreme and whose will is all-embracing.

Almighty God, King of kings, ruler of all creation, give thy people wisdom to discern their duty in this world, and courage never to set it above their duty to thee. Grant to me that I may avoid the snares of thine enemies, and direct my will to follow where true values lead.

The conditions in which it is most easy to live according to the world are those in which it is most difficult to live according to God; and *vice versa*. Nothing is so difficult according to the world than the religious life; nothing is more easy according to God. Nothing is more easy than to have an important appointment and ample means according to the world; nothing is more difficult than to live thus according to God, without taking part in or having a taste for them.

Blaise Pascal (1623–1652) *Thoughts*

Twenty-fourth Sunday after Trinity
Matthew 9.18–26

This is an unusual passage, in that one miracle is described as a passing event in the course of something even greater. Mark and Luke give more detail for both events, strong evidence of an eye-witness account behind the written record. We learn from them that the woman had consulted many physicians without success, that Jesus knew when she touched his garment, and that the accompanying disciples were impatient when he felt her touch in the midst of a jostling crowd. The grieving father is called Jairus, and is a ruler of the local synagogue. Jesus goes into the room with Peter, James and John, and speaks to the little girl. Mark even gives the actual Aramaic words which he spoke, saying 'Little girl, get up.' Here we are told that he went in alone and simply took her by the hand. Matthew may not have been present, and told the essentials of what he had received. What he relates is striking in its simplicity, telling of the power of Jesus to heal and to restore. As we come nearly to the end of the Church year, to read of these acts of love and power sets a seal on the whole ministry in which so many great works were done. Again there is immediate response to words and acts of faith, whether from a man of rank or from a despairing woman. The sceptical jeers of those who stood by do not hinder the divine love. There is encouragement for us in this: persevere in acts of faith even while the world mocks us for them. Consider also the way in which Jesus, going to a distressed family to do a great work, stops to heal an unknown woman in the crowd. How often do we pass by, choose not to notice a need, because we are on the way to somewhere, or do not want to be disturbed? We who think we are living under pressure, are 'stressed out', may yet find a little time to meditate on this Gospel passage. Jesus is stopped on the way to perform one act of compassion, by yet another person in need. He responds to her silent approach, made in desperation and faith. His even greater work is greeted at first with mocking scepticism. Those corrupted by their way of life, equally with the chronically sick, the bereaved and the dead – all receive his healing touch. Jesus does not complain that he is stressed out. His own comfort, his need for rest and food, do not come into question. The infinite love of God is not diminished by the demands of a human body. For most of us, negative responses are probably more frequent than positive unkindness. At the end of the long Trinity season, when Advent is approaching, we may be called to take stock of what is past and make a serious act of self-examination for the time of expectation which is to come. Just a thought for the times when everything seems too much.

O Lord our God, who dost hear the cries of thy people in distress, have mercy on the sick who suffer long, and the families grieved by death. Open my eyes to see, and my ears to hear, that I may respond with love where there is need for my help.

It was a secret matter. There was the whole crowd pressing about Him, begging for a blessing. They did not want it. They were not looking for it. But she did want it, and she felt she wanted it. Nobody knew her. We do not know her name to this day. Only this: among the unknown notables, she is the woman that touched the hem of the Master's garment, and was made whole.

And it is related in three of the Gospels, that you and I may know it as a sweet Gospel story to go right to our hearts. She crept up – nobody knowing her – flung herself down, and just touched the hem of His garment. She said, 'If I may . . . I shall be.' She had faith: and therefore, our Lord crowned her testimony afterwards, and said, 'Thy faith hath made thee whole.'

A. H. Stanton (1839–1913) *Last Sermons in St Alban's, Holborn*

Twenty-fifth Sunday after Trinity
John 6.5–14

Uniquely, a Sunday Gospel is repeated in the yearly cycle. Here we have the same reading as for the Fourth Sunday in Lent, but with the omission of the opening verses. What was written by way of commentary for that Sunday may also be considered for this, with a few further observations. The coming Passover is not mentioned, and perhaps this moves the message away from the Jewish year and association with the Passion, emphasizing more strongly the prefiguring of the Christian Eucharist. Nothing is said about people having followed Jesus to this place, drawn by the miracles which they had witnessed: we see them more as a hungry crowd without expectation of miraculous aid. The narrative begins with Jesus seeing the crowd, without mention of previous withdrawal with his disciples. We should not make too much of the textual shortening, but the Gospel for today does bring us straight into the challenge, the response, and the action which both relieves present physical need and promises future grace. Two additional details may be matter for reflection. Jesus asks Philip how they can get bread, in order to 'prove' him: the sense here is 'test', a challenge to the faith and understanding of a follower who, like all of us, has still much to learn. The remains of the food are to be gathered up, 'that nothing be lost'. It is not a conscientious tidying of the ground, but a symbol of God's enduring care even for what may seem to be unimportant, not used in the great events of the world. Perhaps there is also a lesson for us all in an increasingly wasteful society. Nothing is too small to be the means of God's bountiful love. No one is too insignificant to be a channel of his grace. All we need is faith, and he will do the rest. This Gospel is always to be read on the last Sunday after Trinity, ending the Church year with a strong eucharistic emphasis. Finally, the people see in Jesus the promised great Prophet. The weeks of Advent will renew our understanding that it was God incarnate who came into the world.

Blessed be thy name, most gracious Lord for all thy bountiful gifts, and chiefly for the spiritual food of the Eucharist. Draw me closer to thyself as I prepare for the Advent weeks to come, and mercifully grant that I may never fail in love and reverence towards the holy sacrament.

Christ spoke of buying bread, when he intended to create or make bread; but did He not, in that bread which He made, intend further that Heavenly bread which is the salvation of our souls? – for He goes on to say, 'Labour not for the meat' or food 'which perisheth, but for that food which endureth unto everlasting life, which the Son of man shall give unto you.' Yes, surely the wilderness is the world, and the Apostles are His priests, and the multitudes are His people; and that feast, so suddenly, so unexpectedly provided, is the Holy Communion. He alone is the same, He the provider of the loaves then, of the heavenly manna now. All other things change, but He remaineth.

J. H. Newman (1801–1890) *Parochial and Plain Sermons*

Saints' Days and Major Festivals

St Andrew's Day
Matthew 4.18–22

With St Andrew we begin the Sanctorale, the sequence of commemorations for saints and major festivals, which runs concurrently with the Temporale, the cycle of the Church year which runs from Advent. Andrew was the brother of Simon Peter; he is mentioned several time in the Gospels, although he was not one of the inner circle of Peter, James and John who accompanied Jesus on certain special occasions in his ministry. John introduces him as a disciple of John the Baptist who meets and follows Jesus. Matthew tells of him as a fisherman, called from his work on the Sea of Galilee. The four disciples named in the Gospel for today were not by any means ignorant or unskilled men. They carried on a flourishing trade, including calls on the Gentile side of the lake, which means that they probably spoke sufficient Greek to do business. Mark tells of how James and John followed Jesus, leaving their father Zebedee 'with the hired men', a poignant phrase which suggests a fairly substantial business. The point of this short narrative is that all four men were called while they were fully engaged in their trade. It was not the result of a quiet discussion or a long period of instruction. They were told to follow Jesus and they obeyed at once. It was a strange call: they had developed a skill in one way of life, and now they would have a new target – greater, more demanding, more sacred. Their immediate response has been a beacon to Christians through the ages. All believers are called to serve God in some way, which may mean a complete change of life and perhaps privation and danger. Most have their own less spectacular work to do for the kingdom, no less precious in the sight of God, no less requiring trustful obedience. The call may come to any of us at any time; not perhaps to change a whole way of life, but requiring a response, an act of will which becomes an act of faith. St Andrew's Day falls appropriately at the beginning of Advent, when the call is to be alert, to awake from sleep and be ready for the Lord. We know little of the later life of Andrew; there is a tradition that he carried the gospel into the Gentile world, and that he was martyred. His commemoration has come to be associated with foreign missions, a cause not to be forgotten among the many demands of our time. Andrew was clearly a natural fisherman in more than one sense. Jesus calls him in language that he could well understand, and more than once uses the idea of the net as an image of gathering people into the kingdom. From Galilee to every part of the world, men and women were called to spread the Christian message. The need for preaching the gospel lies all around us, and every Christian is called to mission in a situation of darkness and ignorance in apparently sophisticated circles. We too can fish for people, and we may not have to cast the net very far.

Blessed Lord, whose call has come to thy people in all the ages, inspire us with such zeal for the gospel that we may hear thy voice and follow thy command. Give me grace to hear and to obey, lead me in the way that I should go.

Jesus calls us! O'er the tumult
Of our life's wild restless sea
Day by day his voice is sounding,
Saying, 'Christian, follow me':

As of old Saint Andrew heard it
By the Galilean lake,
Turned from home and toil and kindred.
Leaving all for his dear sake.

Jesus calls us from the worship
Of the vain world's golden store,
From each idol that would keep us,
Saying, 'Christian, love me more'.

In our joys and in our sorrows,
Days of toil and hours of ease,

Still he calls, in cares and pleasures,
'Christian, love me more than these'.

Jesus calls us! By thy mercies,
Saviour, may we hear thy call,
Give our hearts to thy obedience,
Serve and love thee best of all

Cecil Frances Alexander (1818–1895) *New English Hymnal*

St Thomas the Apostle
John 20.24–31

It is unfortunate to be continually stigmatized in popular use
as 'Doubting Thomas'. Having the commemoration four days
before Christmas also means that it becomes obscured, and there
is something to be said for the modern transference to 3 July.
Thomas appears in the Gospels not so much a doubter as an
enquirer and a pessimist. When Jesus is going into the dangerous territory of Judea to raise Lazarus from the dead, Thomas is
prepared to face the worst: 'Let us also go, that we may die with
him' (John 11.16). The men who gathered in the upper room on
the day of resurrection were frightened, meeting behind closed
doors, not convinced by reports of the empty tomb until Jesus
came and gave them the ocular proof. Thomas differed from them
only in demanding the evidence of touch as well as sight, even to
the wound in the side of Jesus, which is recorded only by John
among the Evangelists. Words were not enough, even the words
of trusted friends. The evidence of joy on their faces, the change
from mourning to delight, none of it was enough. Physical evidence, cruel evidence of pain and death, drew from him the confession of divinity. When faith came, it was as wholehearted as
his doubt had been. Personal experience is a vital part of faith.
The Bible and the Church tell us what we need to know but it
does not become an essential part of our being until we have felt
the presence of the Lord. We owe to the reaction of Thomas the

wonderful words of assurance, 'Blessed are they that have not seen, and yet have believed': the promise to Christians through all the ages. It was Thomas who evoked the great 'I am' of Jesus, 'I am the way, the truth and the life', by asking, 'How can we know the way?' (John 14.5, 6). Above all, it was Thomas who uttered the words of faith, 'My Lord and my God', the first human confession of the total divinity of our Lord, and the culmination of the Fourth Gospel. There is indeed a further chapter, in which Thomas is also present, meeting Jesus again on the shore of Galilee. There is an early legend of Thomas going to the East on missionary journeys and suffering martyrdom in India, where the Mar Thoma Church claimed to have been founded by him. But it was Doubting Thomas whose initial scepticism evoked the promise of the perpetual divine presence in the hearts of believers. Thomas was restored to the company of the faithful, but there was a greater blessing for those who came after and know by faith and not by sight that Jesus is Lord and God. The Christian faith has been spread through all lands and in all ages by those who have not seen Christ in the flesh but have experienced his risen presence. God depends on us to be his witnesses in our time. Still there are many who would like to believe, but hold back because it seems too good to be true, a fairy story, a wish fulfilment. Only those who have tried to suffer in spirit with Jesus, who have followed him with devotion from the manger to the cross, can know the resurrection joy and tell the world, 'We have seen the Lord.'

Dear Lord, who dost reveal thyself to thy people through the eyes of faith and the experience of thy love, strengthen and confirm the faith in me, forgive my doubts and my failures of trust, and let me always reverence the wounds which were suffered for my sake.

Why did Thomas not believe? And why are so many of us Christians unable to realise their condition and privileges? It is much the same reason in both cases. Our own senses, our own experiences, do not confirm what we are called on to believe. St Thomas was told by his fellow-disciples that they had seen the Lord, but his timid spirit was not content with their report:

he wanted to see him his own self, to see his Wounds, and not only to see, but to feel them: then, he said, he could believe, but not otherwise. So we Christians are taught in the Catechism that we are 'members of Christ, children of God, and inheritors of the kingdom of heaven', but we do not see it, nor feel it: we see and feel the same as unbaptized people do. The world is about us, as it is about them, with its wants and pains and cares and pleasures; and there is in too many of us an evil heart of unbelief, a sullen obstinate spirit. If we could see with our eyes such things the Apostles saw, heaven opened, the dead raised, all sorts of miracles wrought, then perhaps, we think we should believe: but as it is, we do not, and cannot. We walk by sight, not by faith: see what we lose by it.

John Keble (1792–1866) *Sermons for Saints' Days*

The Conversion of St Paul
Matthew 19.27–30

We need to read the passage from the Acts of the Apostles, which is the Epistle for today, in connection with the Gospel. The story of the conversion of Paul – or rather of Saul, later to change his name – is well known but so remarkable that we need to be continually reminded of it. Here was an ultra-orthodox Jew, a member of the Pharisees who had been among the most persistent opponents of Jesus, a man given a specific commission to root out and destroy the new movement. Stopped in his tracks as he pursued the way of anger and destruction, he met his Master on the road. It is no wonder that the followers of Jesus at first suspected him: as if a Gestapo officer had come seeking fellowship with a Jewish community. Later he would meet others who shared the faith but differed from him in some requirements, and give to them the right hand of friendship. This man undertook many missionary journeys, often with perils beyond the usual hazards of travel at that time, and became the first Christian theologian through the letters which he wrote to the new churches. Peter's rather brash question about future rewards falls into place for this day. The Gospels often give indications of what was to come, and here the disciples, and all who would later follow in that way, are told of what must be forsaken and what will be gained. Our faith calls on all of us to give up something for Christ: for some a major sacrifice, for most a certain discipline of life and positive action. Those who look to the cross find joy after suffering, life after death to some of the things of this world. Paul gave up everything for the Lord, who kept him steadfast to the end. Peter still had much to learn, but he too was sustained and strengthened. Following Christ from our first years, accepting him later in life or even near life's end, are all pleasing to God. We remember the parable of the Labourers in the Vineyard and the message repeated here that the first shall be last and the last first. Let us try in our small way to find some of Paul's missionary zeal. Our earthly hierarchies have no status in the kingdom, but the life everlasting will have joys that we cannot yet conceive. Saul the persecutor became Paul the apostle, sharing the suffering of those whom he had wanted to destroy. A late convert became a missionary to his own people and to the despised Gentiles outside the Law. God's power to change lives and to heal wounds has not left us. The feast of St Paul is the focus of the Week of Prayer for Christian Unity. May the Spirit who made enemies into friends draw into one those who love the Lord of love. The call of God may come early or late in life, but when it comes the change is greater than anything the human will could choose.

Thanks be to thee O God for the faith and work of blessed Paul, and for the power which gave strength to him and to the faithful who have been called through all the years. Forgive my weakness, my lack of zeal in bringing others to thee, and empower me to impart the glorious news of salvation which I have received.

The wise then, turn their eyes toward the One who is their head, but fools grope in darkness. No one who puts a lamp under a bed instead of on a lampstand will receive any light from it. People are often considered blind and useless when they make the supreme Good their aim and give themselves up to the contemplation of God, but Paul made a boast of this and proclaimed himself a fool for Christ's sake. The reason he said, 'We are fools for Christ's sake,' was that his mind was free from all earthly preoccupations. It was as though he said, 'We are blind to the life here below because our eyes are raised toward the One who is our head.'

Gregory of Nyssa (c 340–c 394) 'On Ecclesiastes', *Homilies* 5

The Presentation of Christ in the Temple
Luke 2.22–40

This day has also been known as the Purification, recognizing the command in the Jewish Law which required a mother to make her offering for a newborn child. It has left its seal on our liturgy in the order for the Churching of Women, now much neglected but not to be forgotten. Our focus this day is upon Jesus who was brought to the Temple. The Gospel records the obedience of Mary and Joseph, doing all that was necessary to affirm the true manhood of the Son who was also truly divine. They did not try to use the angelic messages as a way of escaping their religious duty. The small offering of birds was a permitted alternative to the more costly lamb, for those who were not rich; all is done with quiet and humility. Unknown as yet, it was the true Lamb of God who was that day being presented. But this time the routine ceremony was marked by strange happenings. Simeon and Anna saw that this was no ordinary child and gave their testimony to the glory of God. Wonderful words are spoken, looking to the great things which God's purpose will reveal. They are spoken not by priests or prophets but by two devout old people without any status in the religious hierarchy. Simeon is granted a vision of salvation not only for his own people, but also for the whole world with which the Temple authorities would have had no dealings. He sees the light which has come into the world: this feast is sometimes called

Candlemas and celebrated with many lights. Simeon foresees also the opposition which Jesus will arouse by his words and deeds, and warns Mary of the sorrow she will suffer. His words give us the canticle Nunc Dimittis, said or sung at Evening Prayer, and often spoken at the end of a funeral. The old widow Anna is also moved to utter praise and speak of redemption to come. There is so much for us to receive and honour in this marvellous event, after which there is silence in the Gospels until the Finding in the Temple, as the holy family lives quietly in Nazareth. When the promise of the Messiah was fulfilled, few could recognize him in a human child. The vision of one man was the beginning of the revelation to come. Simeon asked no more from life. He was ready to go, leaving the world to a greater act of divine love than his people had ever dreamed of, even through their inspired prophets. For 40 days we have celebrated the incarnation. Now the time is fulfilled, the duty is performed, and we turn to look towards the cross. The words of Simeon remain, an assurance that it is never too late to see the glory of the Lord.

We too can be quiet and listen to the words which were spoken in the Temple. The calm and joyful desire of Simeon to depart in peace is the pattern for the faithful followers of Jesus. We might also remember that the words of simple, unregarded people around us can contain much vision and wisdom.

Blessed art thou, O God, for the revelation of the Son as a light to the whole world. Grant that I may ever walk by that light, bring light to others, and come in faith to the light of eternal life after the darkness of bodily death.

Because of his righteousness God revealed to him while he was still in the body, that he would not depart this present transitory life until his own arms had enfolded Life Eternal, our Lord Jesus Christ. Simeon the righteous, who before the incarnation had longed to see the Lord, saw him incarnate, recognized him, and took him in his arms. Then he cried for release from the prison of his body, calling as a servant on the Lord of all who appeared as a child, 'Now, Lord, you let your servant go in peace as you promised, for my eyes have seen your salvation'. I have seen, allow me to leave, do not keep me here. Let me depart in peace, do not keep me in distress. I have seen, let me go: I have seen your glory, seen the angels dancing, the archangels praising you, creation leaping for joy, a way made between heaven and earth. Now let me depart, do not keep me here below.

Timothy of Jerusalem (*fl.* 400) *Oratio in Symeonem*

St Matthias's Day
Matthew 11.23–30

We need to complete the observance of this day by reading the account of the choosing of Matthias as an apostle in Acts 1.15–26. The gap left by the suicide of Judas was filled before the Holy Spirit came upon them at Pentecost. The band of twelve seems to have corresponded to the twelve tribes of Israel. The selection by drawing lots may seem strange to our modern mind, but it has precedents in the Old Testament as a way of calling on God for guidance. More importantly for our understanding, we are reminded that the Twelve often named as disciples of Jesus were not his only close followers. It was not a question of one small group as in contrast with vague crowds who came and went when miracles were performed. It is made clear that a good number had been close to Jesus, faithfully from the coming of John the Baptist to the ascension, and that there were more witnesses to the risen Christ than appear in the Gospel accounts. We know that at one point 70 were sent out as missionaries to testify to the great works already done and call people to belief. Jesus opened the wisdom of God to many and, as today's Gospel records, gave thanks for the simple faith aroused in those who seemed far from the scholars and official teachers. Then as now, ordinary and seemingly unlikely people were being called to the greatest service. Jesus speaks of how the Father is revealed not by human effort but by the mediation of the Son. God is beyond any conception we can have of time, but we may say in human terms that he gets his timing right. There is no trace of Matthias, or the other candidate Justus, until the moment came. It is one of the many examples in Scripture of what is called in Greek '*kairos*', the significant moment when something of importance is revealed and calls for a response. With the choosing of Matthias, the gap is filled, the wound is healed. He appears for a moment and then is lost to view – not another word of him in the Acts of the Apostles – nothing else but legends and the use of his name for a lost Gospel. But if he was called and chosen, there will have been work for him to do. Numbered among the apostles, in history and in commemoration, he is the hope of all who find a late vocation, or who come to the Christian faith after many years of doubt and unbelief. He leaves no place for regrets about the wasted years, no resentment about a promising start that brings no fame. His brief story is one that many can understand. Then and now, there may seem to be loss, individual or collective damage that causes such distress, but in his time God provides the remedy. It is a small figure of the wonderful way in which the death and resurrection of Jesus healed the wound of human sin. This day's Gospel ends with the beautiful call to accept the yoke of Jesus and find it no burden, but rest and peace. Somewhere, at every instant, someone finds the peace of God which passes all understanding. We think that we have our priorities and our ways of deciding what is to be done. God sometimes works against all our expectations and brings to fruition something that we had not imagined.

Almighty God, by whose holy will all things are ordered, all faults corrected and all wounds healed, give peace to thy people when they are troubled and perplexed. Strengthen me to feel the assurance of thy love and to follow thee in calm obedience.

The reflection which rises in the mind on a consideration of the election of St Matthias is this: how easily God may effect his purposes without us, and put others in our place, if we are disobedient to him. It often happens that those who have long been in his favour grow secure and presuming. They think their salvation certain, and their service necessary to him who has graciously accepted it. They consider themselves as personally bound up with his purposes of mercy manifested in the Church, and so marked out that, if they could fall, his word would fail. They come to think they have some peculiar title or interest in his promises, over and above other men (however derived, it matters not, whether from his eternal decree, or, on the other hand, from their own especial holiness and obedience) but practically such an interest that the very supposition that they can possibly fall offends them. Now, this feeling of self-importance is repressed all through the Scriptures, and especially by the events we commemorate today.

J. H. Newman (1801–1890) *Parochial and Plain Sermons*

The Annunciation of the Blessed Virgin Mary
Luke 1.26–38

It is not surprising that the annunciation has been a favourite subject for painters. It is a highly dramatic story in human terms, and a pivotal moment in God's eternal purpose. Angels as messengers of God appear in the Old Testament and continue to hold their place in the popular imagination, while giving the believer deeper thought about the mysteries of the whole creation. It started as an ordinary day when Mary did not expect anything special to happen. Angels had come to some favoured ones in the stories that she knew, but she did not expect any of them to pass through her home town. Perhaps she was thinking of her coming marriage to Joseph. The sequence of Mary's response is something that we can understand when we think about receiving strange and disturbing news, but magnified by the presence of the angelic visitor. First there is fear, anxiety about words which seem to cut through all previous experience. Then the message itself brings incredulity: how can this virgin woman be promised a child? The simple human fact for a moment seems as startling as the prophecy of who this child will be. Reassurance comes from within the family, for her aged cousin

Elizabeth is already three months pregnant: as ever, God is working through people as they are and as they can understand. Then come acceptance, trusting submission to the will of God, the role of a servant in this great mystery. The work of redemption is about to begin, from the Nativity to the cross and the resurrection. Yet we may say that this is Mary's Day, 'Lady Day' as it was traditionally known. She accepted the divine will and began to form the human body of the Redeemer, the Son of God. She would nurture him, protect him, lose and find him, see him grow to manhood and a wandering life, see him at last in the agony of death when a sword pierced her own soul. Mary: honoured in the sequence of the Church year; sometimes extravagantly worshipped beyond what Scripture and early tradition can offer; sometimes by reaction ignored and scarcely remembered. This is the day when history changed, when the long years of promise were fulfilled and the new Covenant would begin; and at its centre is a young woman sitting in a house in a small Galilean town, alone until the angel is suddenly present. She accepted the word and believed the promise. With the whole story now laid out before us, with the fellowship of the Church, and with each individual experience of God's love, how can we show anything less than Mary's simple faith? We praise God today for his loving purpose, for the salvation of the human race through the response of people called to do his will.

Praise be to thee, O God, for the wonderful coming of thy Son into the world, to take our flesh and to suffer death for our salvation. Grant me the loving obedience of Mary, chosen to be the mother of the Saviour, and give me grace always to hear and receive thy word for me.

There is no fact in the New Testament more particularly given. The name of the angel is given – Gabriel. God sent His angel to a maiden. The name of the maiden is given – Mary, espoused to Joseph, of the tribe of Judah. The name of the place is given. Every little particular conceivable about the Incarnation of the Son of God, it is all given, word for word. You read it in your Bibles, exactly as it were, to answer the faithlessness of the age.

And when Mary is troubled, as naturally the maiden would be troubled, at the stupendous secret told her, the angel assures her, 'Fear not'. And the angel tells her, the angel actually tells her exactly how it will happen. 'The power of the Highest shall overshadow thee, therefore that Holy Thing that shall be born of thee shall be called the Son of God'. It is told so that you and I can have no sort of doubt about the matter. The Holy Ghost has revealed everything fully.

A.H. Stanton (1839–1913) *Last Sermons in St Alban's, Holborn*

St Mark's Day
John 15.1–11

Mark's Gospel is the shortest, and generally greed to be the first of the four Gospels, and one of the sources on which Matthew and Luke drew, and probably the first to use the word *'euangelion'*, 'good news' in its new Christian sense. Mark does not himself appear in the account of the earthly life of Jesus, although it is possible that he left a personal memory in the young man who fled away naked in the Garden of Gethsemane, an episode which only this Gospel mentions (Mark 14.51). He was with Paul on a missionary journey until they separated after a dispute, and by tradition he became a companion of Peter, and recorded his memories. His Gospel, often economical in its narrative, several times gives details absent in the others, which suggest the memory of an eyewitness. He was not one of the Twelve, but his record made him one of the most valuable members of the early Church. Soon the good news was being proclaimed. In time, Mark's words would be translated into languages and declared to nations of whom he had not heard. Their voice, as the psalmist says, has gone out into all the world. The great work has not been left only to those whose lives have been devoted to it. In ordinary conversation, in argument and confrontation, in the quiet time of people who are close to one another, the good news can be proclaimed. In the Gospel for today, Jesus uses an image which will be familiar even to the least expert of modern gardeners. We all know that a broken branch is useless and has to be disposed of, and all that grows, from the tender plant to the mighty oak, depends for life on its central stem. In the same way, we are all joined with our Lord for whatever task he has called us, and we can do nothing without his grace and power. When we think we are self-sufficient, secure in our own strength, able to resist temptation by our unaided will, disaster is sure to follow. It is the great love continually poured out from its divine source that sustains us and supplies all that is lacking in our weakness. The love which brought Jesus to the cross did not end with the victory of his Passion. It fills the world now and for ever, until all things are brought to their end. It empowers the Church through all its members, whether famous theologians, missionaries, or simple believers who know their need and where to find the remedy. Mark had a mighty call and he answered it in the grace that was given him, and for the instruction of generations to come. Let us think today of all who spread the word by writing or teaching, or by their own deeds of love. Let us pray for them, and for our own calling whatever it may be. It is in the purpose of God that the good news of the kingdom should be known to all. In his wisdom, he works through all kinds of men and women to be his chosen messengers.

And let us remember too that even the most fruitful branches sometimes need pruning. We may have to lose something before we can continue to bear the good fruit of the Gospel.

Heavenly Father, who dost sustain and enable thy Church by the strength of the everlasting Vine, keep thy children firm in the faith delivered through the holy Gospels. Guide me in the way of truth, cleanse me from all that is false, make me a channel of thy love in the world.

O my noble vine, give Thou Thy branch sap, that I may grow and flourish in Thine essence, by Thy power and nourishment. O sweet Love, art Thou not my Light? Lighten Thou my poor soul during her doleful imprisonment in flesh and blood. Lead

her always by the right way. Break Thou the will of the Evil
One, and lead Thou my body through the course of this world,
through the chamber of death, into Thy death and peace, that
it may, at the last day, arise in Thee out of Thy death, and live
eternally in Thee. Teach Thou me what I should do, be Thou
my willing, my knowing, and my doing, and let me go nowhere
without Thee. I devote myself utterly unto Thee.

Jacob Behmen (1575–1624) 'The Way to Christ', *Thought on
the Spiritual Life*

St Philip and St James's Day
John 14.1–14

These two saints have been joined in church lectionaries for many
centuries, there being no certain reason. Philip appears several
times in the Fourth Gospel: as an early disciple, is tested before the
miraculous feeding, introduces some Gentile enquirers to Jesus, and
at the Last Supper makes the request recorded in today's Gospel,
'Show us the Father.' We know little about James, described as 'Son
of Alphaeus' and sometimes called 'James the Less'. If the saints
were like us, we could imagine some grumbling in heaven about
having to share a special day, and perhaps about being called 'Less'.
We may trust that the blessed ones have shed any petty human
weaknesses. Philip's request to Jesus opens a new window of revelation for the disciples, and for those who will come to share the
record of their lives. To know Jesus is to know all that we can
know of God within our limited earthly understanding. To have
seen him, whether with the eyes of the body or the eyes of faith, is
to behold the divine. In him there is all we know or need to know
in this world, about the very nature of God, partly revealed by
glimpses under the old Covenant, fully revealed in the new. The
disciples are still not confident; they are distressed to learn that their
Master is going away, but he reassures them. The realm of God has
'many mansions', many dwelling-places, or places to stop and rest.

He who has loved his followers in this world will have a place made for each of them in the world to come. The compassionate love which has healed physical and spiritual troubles in this world will also enfold us in the next. It is the comfort of Christians to know that what is death to us is the receiving into a new life, united again with the Master we have loved and trusted, however imperfect our efforts. Philip and James may not have been the most prominent of the disciples, but they were equally charged and empowered to hear, witness and tell. The great commission is also for each of us if we will accept it. The full glory of God, announced by the prophets, was revealed in Jesus Christ. There is sadness in the words of Jesus: 'Have I been so long with you, yet thou hast not known me, Philip?' It is always sad to find that one whom you thought was intimate does not really know you as you are. There are still many who respect Jesus Christ as a teacher of morality, or as a pattern of loving human warmth, but fail to know him fully. Even his disciples did not understand; their ignorance should make us guard against failing fully to recognize his divinity.

Glory be to thee, O God, for all thy saints who have borne witness to the divinity of the Lord Jesus. Help me to follow in that faith, and to live in the confidence that a place in eternal life is prepared for all who have believed the promise.

'Does the road wind up-hill all the way?'
'Yes, to the very end.'
'Will the day's journey take the whole long day?'
'From morn to night, my friend.'

'But is there for the night a resting-place?'
'A roof for when the slow dark hours begin.'
'May not the darkness hide it from my face?'
'You cannot miss that inn.'

'Shall I meet other wayfarers at night?'
'Those who have gone before.'
'Then must I knock, or call when just in sight?'
'They will not keep you standing at that door.'

'Shall I find comfort, travel-sore and weak?'
'Of labour you shall find the sum.'
'Will there be beds for me and all who seek?'
'Yea. Beds for all who come.'

Christina Rossetti (1830–1894) 'Up-Hill', *Poems*

St Barnabas the Apostle
John 15.12–16

As there were more close followers of Jesus during his earthly
ministry than the named Twelve, so more than the original twelve
apostles were called as the Church began to grow. Barnabas came
early into their number, one of those who sold land or goods
and gave money to the needs of the Church. He brought Paul,
newly converted but still a cause of fear, to be accepted by the
faithful. He accompanied Paul on his first missionary journey and
was powerful as a preacher of the gospel which was beginning to
spread across the Roman world. They went together to what is
known as the Council of Jerusalem, when the apostles debated
whether Gentile converts should be required to conform to Jewish
laws and customs. Both men spoke of what God had done among
the Gentiles, and it was agreed that there were no racial barriers
to full membership of the Church: a great moment in its history.
Barnabas was in fact one of those so valuable to the Church and
indeed to many human associations: a peacemaker, an intermedi-
ary in problems, wise in judgement, zealous for what he believed.
In fact he fulfilled the command of love which Jesus gave in his
long discourse on the evening before his Passion. As far as we
know he wrote no letters to the new converts, did not expound
points of doctrine or found any new local churches. His ministry
was quiet, loving, constant. Those who love and follow Jesus are
received as friends, not as servants, granted a status beyond all
deserving. We must always remember that we are members of
God's Church not by our own unaided choice but by response to
his calling. Being a Christian is not like deciding to join a club or

support a political party. It is the free gift of grace which brings with it the duty to respond to love by love, remembering that Jesus spoke of laying down his life for his friends, and that he laid down his life not only for his friends, but for the whole human race. The Church today, still seeking unity and still composed of very fallible individuals, also needs people like this – a Barnabas in every parish or church community would not be excessive. Sometimes the leaders seem too busy to remember the Lord's great command to love one another; it is good that he still raises up women and men for the less spectacular works of reconciliation. To work for peace and reconciliation is one of the most blessed Christian ministries. Suspicion and hostility can be removed by love better than by confrontation. Can we in our smaller way help to bring people to God as Barnabas did? And for today and all days, remember that love is the central word in the two great commandments as Jesus gave them.

God of love, Giver of all good gifts, who callest us not for our merits but by thy grace alone, accept my praise for my calling, empower me to do thy work, and fill me with thine own generous love to thee and to others.

We go to bring forth, and He Himself is the way wherein we go, and wherein He hath appointed us to go. Accordingly let love remain; for He Himself is our fruit. And this love lies at present in longing desire, not yet in fullness of enjoyment; and whatsoever with that longing desire we shall ask in the name of the only-begotten Son, the Father giveth us.

Augustine (354–430) *Homily on the Gospel of John*

St John Baptist's Day
Luke 1.57–80

Those who have suffered death in the service of God are usually remembered on the day of their martyrdom. For John the Baptist, we celebrate his birth, which the Gospel relates in detail. John is born only a few months before Jesus, his cousin after the flesh, whom he will in due time recognize and proclaim. He is born to an elderly mother who seemed to have no prospect of children. His birth is announced by an angel to a devout but sceptical father who loses his speech until the actual birth, when he can give the name which surprises the rest of the family. Zacharias then utters the song of praise and prophecy which we know in our Morning Prayer as the Benedictus. These are great signs, even as greater ones are about to come in Bethlehem. Then John and Jesus pass for years from the record, growing up quietly to manhood until the time comes for the declaration of God's purpose. John comes baptizing and calling to repentance, a wild, commanding figure. He is like the last of the Old Testament prophets, and the first believer in the Son of God, whose shoe he does not feel worthy to touch. The Benedictus tells of how God spoke through the prophets, and it is a cogent reminder for us that our faith has deep roots in the Jewish Scriptures. That which we call the New Testament gives all that we need for faith and obedience, but we do not understand it in all its fullness if we neglect the Old. God reveals himself in many ways, and calls all kinds of people to his service. Can we proclaim the good news as forcefully as John did, while treating others with tact and Christian love? Not an easy task, but the record of the Baptist should strengthen us to know where help is to be found. Elizabeth and Zechariah waited a long time for a child, but when one came it was with great signs and marvels. The centuries of preparation were over and the divine light was coming into the world. The promises of God are not always met with the faith and obedience of Zechariah. There is a preference for the easier way, the familiar solution, doing what has always been done before. But from that day to this lives are being prepared for service which is to be revealed when the time comes. There may not always be much significance in a name, but there is no telling what is being offered as a token of obedi-ence. The long unfolding of the Old Testament tells how God's time is not our time, but it reveals his purpose as and when he wills for us.

God, who didst inspire the prophets and guide thy people of the old Covenant, give to those who have received the new Covenant wisdom to learn from the deep roots of their faith. May I find the zeal of John the Baptist and lead others to the way of salvation.

Hail, harbinger of morn:
Thou that art this day born,
And heraldest the Word with clarion voice!
Ye faithful ones, in him
Behold the dawning dim
Of the bright day, and let your hearts rejoice

John – by that chosen name
To call him, Gabriel came
By God's appointment from his home on high:
What deeds that babe should do
To manhood when he grew,
God sent his angel forth to testify.

Bede (673–735) *New English Hymnal*

St Peter's Day
Matthew 16.13–19

Peter is the most prominent member of the Twelve as recorded in the Gospels. He is usually the first to speak, asking questions, or failing to understand the teaching of Jesus. He is impetuous in deed as well as in speech, rushing into the empty tomb, jumping into the water when the risen Lord appears on the shore. He is the first to promise to follow Jesus even to death, and then three times denies knowing him. At the last his love is challenged, tested and accepted and he is given his charge for the new Church, where he has a leading part which by tradition led to his martyrdom at Rome. Perhaps we find some pleasure when the Gospel for his yearly commemoration finds him getting it right and being commended by his Master. He is the first to acknowledge who Jesus really is, to end in one sentence all the doubt and conjecture. Jesus had already given him the name Cephas which in Aramaic, or Peter in Greek, means 'rock', and in spite of his weaknesses he is to be a strong foundation for the Church. We need not here try to determine whether the power was given specially to him above all the other apostles: it is enough to know that witnesses were sent out with the great commission to take the gospel everywhere. When Peter made his declaration at Caesarea Philippi, people were still confused and uncertain about Jesus and even his closest disciples were uncertain. Was he John the Baptist returned to life, or a reappearance of one of the old Covenant prophets? Many today are still uncertain, willing to accept Jesus as a teacher of morals and an example of human love, but not recognizing him as the divine Saviour of the world. We may not be great pillars of the Church, but do we perceive and know in ourselves something like the life of Peter? Faith which often falls short, mistakes and rash judgements, times when we seem to have denied our Lord, the joy of continual pardon and fresh opportunities – these are the Christian experience in this world. God gives great revelations even to the most fallible of his children. The loudest voice of those who promised to follow Jesus even to death, and three times denied knowing him: it is a record that would make a selector for the ordained ministry feel very dubious. But God does not always choose those who have already proved their ability and leadership. He does not see with our limited vision, but knows the hidden gifts that can be drawn into his service. Where a human employer or trainer would have given up, Jesus patiently worked on the man until he was made new. Even later Peter was still sometimes hesitant, changing his opinions according to his company, but basically he was the solid rock of faith. Glory this day to God who knew where to find, under the weakness and the folly, one of his greatest apostles. And if we are open to him, he can make something of each one of us.

Almighty God, who hast in all ages called men and women to thy service, continue in thy Church the promise made to blessed Peter for the strength of faith and the pardon of sin. Preserve me from the errors and weakness of this mortal life, grant that I may never fail thee or deny thee by word or deed, but may stand firm in faith until the end.

Jesus waited, He laboured, He prayed in our true manhood till He had prepared the soil which should be adequate for the seed He meant to sow in it; till He had found a foundation, not like the shifting sand of ordinary fallen manhood, but strong and rock-like, on which He could build; and this rock-like character our human nature was to gain only through faith in Himself complete and entire. Thus, when He had gained from the lips of St Peter an adequate confession of His name, a confession different altogether from the vague and shifting ideas about Himself which were current among the people generally, then it was that He could make a beginning with His new spiritual structure. He turned to Peter, the representative of the new confession, and said, 'Blessed art thou, Simon Bar-Jonah; for flesh and blood hath not revealed it unto thee, but my Father which is in heaven. And I also say unto thee, that thou art Peter – Rockman – and upon this rock I will build my church, and the gates of death shall not prevail against it.'

Charles Gore (1852–1932) *The Mission of the Church*

St James the Apostle
Matthew 20.20–28

There are several mentions of the names James and John in the New Testament, sometimes easily confused. Today is the commemoration of James the son of Zebedee, one of the Twelve and brother of John with whom he is usually associated in the Gospels. Peter, James and John seem to have been the inner circle who were called to be with Jesus at certain times, such as the transfiguration and the raising of the daughter of Jairus. James is mentioned before John on these occasions and may have been the elder brother, but in the early chapters of the Acts of the Apostles, it is John who comes to prominence and is the companion of Peter in works of preaching and healing. The wife of Zebedee seems to have been a notable example of the embarrassing mother, drawing attention to her wish for special privileges for her sons. However, the brothers are ready to accept her intervention and to respond confidently to the challenging question which Jesus puts to them, It was not for nothing that Jesus had earlier called them Boanerges, 'Sons of thunder'. They do not yet know that the baptism to be shared is the baptism of innocent blood, that the cup is not only the cup of salvation but also the bitter cup of death. Then the other ten join in the discussion, indignant that these two should be singled out. In fact, it is a very human situation, escalating from family pride to a general falling out. The whole group needed to be called together and reminded that the values of the kingdom are not the values of this world. Jesus had given them the supreme example of humility and service, and again he told them of his coming sacrificial death. They did not yet fully understand his purpose, and they had not grasped the cost of taking up the cross and following him. James was martyred by Herod Agrippa during the early persecution of the Church. From this rather unedifying episode we may learn to beware of selfishness in spiritual as well as material things. There are no prizewinners in the great company of ransomed sinners: true greatness lies in thankfulness and humble service. Following Jesus is the highest of privileges, but it can be costly and demanding. Let us not seek for extra privileges either for ourselves or for those we love. Self-confidence may be a useful gift in getting on socially and professionally but it can be a disaster in the life of faith. The way of Christ leads to joy and also to sorrow, for to share his love is also to share his suffering. It is not for reward in this world or the next that we must follow him. James got it right at last, and we may be thankful for the warning of his first error.

Keep, O Lord, thy people from the snare of pride and ambition. Make me always ready to serve thee, to follow the pattern of divine humility shown in perfect humanity, and give me the desire and the strength to live according to thy loving will for me.

Lord, who shall sit beside thee,
Enthroned on either hand
When clouds no longer hide thee,
'Mid all thy faithful band?
Who drinks the cup of sorrow
Thy Father gave to thee
'Neath shadows of the morrow
In dark Gethsemane;

Who on thy Passion thinking
Can find in loss a gain,
And dare to meet unshrinking
Thy baptism of pain.

William Romanis (1824–1899) *New English Hymnal*

St Bartholomew the Apostle
Luke 22.24–30

We know hardly anything about Bartholomew; he may be the same as Nathaniel, who was brought to Jesus by Philip. It is perhaps rather hard on him that, because he has no individual place in the Gospel, he is remembered on his special day as being involved in a general dispute about status. It is much the same problem as the theme for James: jealousy and worldly ambition among the disciples. But whereas the previous account was one of general indignation against James, John and their mother, now we find them all arguing and getting into a most unedifying quarrel. Having shared the privilege of being close to Jesus, witnessing his miracles and hearing his special teaching, the Twelve think that there should be some ranking among them, some special status which each of them wants to claim. The particular sadness about this dispute is that it happens at the Last Supper, a few hours before their Master will make the ultimate act of humility and service by the sacrifice of the cross. He has to remind them of the way in which he has walked with them, and with the people of his country, without privilege or deference.

They have been faithful, stayed with him, shared the trials and testing of three years in wandering ministry and frugal living: surely they will not fail now. Sadly, we know that very soon when the time of truth comes, they will forsake him and run away. Jesus promises them that they will indeed have their reward, but it will not be as the world sees these things. In the kingdom of God earthly values are overthrown. The humble are closest to the divine example; the first may be last and the last first; suffering, not luxury, is the result of obedience. The feasts of James and Bartholomew offer us much to learn if we will accept it. Evidence of the temptations of power and influence, whether in a small circle of acquaintances or on an international level, is all around us. In God's mercy, few will be driven down the road to power that leads to suffering for others. But minor ambitions are too often found in church circles. The Twelve were men specially called, eventually to be given a strength not their own as apostles, but they could be prey to false values and petty jealousies. The little band who walked with Jesus represents the whole company of Christian people. If some of them were chosen to be with him at special times, or if they feature more often in the Gospel stories, they are not to feel more important but rather to seek the lowest place. Rank, achievement, even good works, fall away before the sacrificial love that gives new life. Christians are those who know their need, and rely on nothing but the mercy and grace of God. We know nothing about Bartholomew except that he was called and that he obeyed. His gift to us on his feast day is the reminder that the call of God is not to honour but to humility.

Glory be to thee, O Lord, for the pattern of divine service and the sacrifice made even for the proud and ungracious. Teach me day by day to know the way of my spiritual journey and to follow it in obedience and trust.

When impulses of anger and envy towards your fellow-Christians rise in your heart, examine and watch yourself closely. The stronger these feelings and the more you are moved to gloomy bitterness or ill-will, the more impatiently you grumble, whether against God because of any trouble, sickness, or infirmity he sends you, or against your fellow-Christians, the less is the likeness of Jesus reformed in you. I do not say that such grumblings and instinctive reactions are mortal sins, but I do say that they prevent purity of heart and quietness of conscience. As a result you cannot attain to perfect charity, which is essential to the contemplative life. My purpose in all that I say is that you should not only cleanse your heart from all mortal sins, but also as far as possible from venial sins, so that by the grace of Jesus Christ the sources of sin within you may be removed. For although you may feel no ill-will towards your fellow-Christians for a time, you cannot be sure that the sources of sin within you are destroyed, because you are not yet in full possession of the virtue of charity.

Walter Hilton (1340–1396) *The Ladder of Perfection*

St Matthew the Apostle
Matthew 9.9–12

Matthew has been regarded as the author of the first Gospel included in the New Testament, though not the first to be written. There is plenty of room for discussion and opinion about authorship, but we have here a record which tells us many precious things about the life and teaching of our Lord. It is a Gospel which shows much knowledge of the Jewish Scriptures, and often relates the teaching of Jesus to the words of the tradition. Busy about his daily work, not much troubled by what his fellow-citizens were thinking of him, it seemed like an ordinary day for Matthew – or Levi as he is also called. His summons to be a disciple is the more remarkable because he was a tax-gatherer. He was not like a modern official of the Inland Revenue, honest if not always deeply loved. He was collecting taxes or custom dues on behalf of an alien occupying power. Such men, who bought a franchise for taxes and made the best profit they could, were numbered among sinners by the righteous Jews of the time. Had he seen Jesus before, was he already partly convicted in his conscience, or was this the first encounter? We do not know, but a simple command as the Master passed by was enough to change a life. Like the fishermen called by the Sea of Galilee, he is given the word to follow Jesus when he is occupied in his work, and like them he immediately obeys. Others who were rejected and ostracized by the religious establishment joined Jesus and the disciples at the meal, called and reassured by the feeling of unconditional love. As usual, the Pharisees are outraged and challenge the disciples for joining their Master in company of the unclean. This gives Jesus the opening for one of his greatest sayings. It is those sick from sin who need his pardoning love, and he has come so that they may know repentance and new life. Always, then and now, it may be that those who are most sure of their righteousness are most lacking it, those who feel themselves rejected who are the nearest to the heart of God. Many think that Christians are 'good people who go to church'. But Christians are sinners who know their need, and where to find the remedy. They do not trust in their own strength, but cast all their care upon the Holy One who cares for them. The calling of Matthew is one of the greatest warnings to avoid self-righteousness and to find Jesus in places and in company which may seem unexpected. He responded at once to the voice of the Lord. Whether it comes in a moment of conversion or in continuing calling back when we have gone astray, we must pray to do no less. Matthew's shrewdness and skill may have sometimes been useful for the band of disciples, but there was only childlike trust and the knowledge of irresistible grace, when he first got up and followed Jesus.

Lord of mercy, friend of sinners, healer of souls, look with mercy on all who have gone astray and have not turned to thy love. Grant me such holy wisdom that, knowing my need, I may hear and respond to thy call, trusting not in myself but in thy strength alone.

Why, all the souls that were, were forfeit once,
And he that might the vantage best have took
Found out the remedy. How would you be
If he, which is the top of judgement, should

But judge you as you are? O think on that,
And mercy then will breed within your lips,
Like man new made.

William Shakespeare (1564–1616) *Measure for Measure*

St Michael and all Angels
Matthew 18.1–10

Angels make several appearances in both the Old and the New Testaments, usually brief but significant. A higher order in creation than humanity, they come as messengers or helpers, or as assurance of God's purpose. Gabriel comes to Mary at the annunciation; angels rejoice at the Nativity. Michael is one of the few angels actually named in the Bible, seen as the protector of Christians against the forces of evil. He has the role of God's warrior, notably in the overthrow of the devil and his allies (Revelation 12.7–9). The early Church thought of nine orders for these celestial beings, with Michael among the archangels. The Gospel for this day focuses on human weakness, so different from the pure service of the angels. The Twelve are at it again, concerned about rank and power, projecting human aspiration on the kingdom of heaven. Jesus has told them about taking the role of a servant, and now he gives them a living example of what it means to follow him. Looking upon the innocence and trust of a little child, their false ambitions are challenged and put to shame. The values of this world are not the values of the kingdom. The lesson is not only for humility, but also for the duty which is owed to children, then and for ever. Through his wonderful incarnation, Jesus is present in every child, and every child is to be received as if it were the Lord himself. Love and care of children is one of the highest privileges which we are offered. More darkly, there is a strong warning about the utter evil of offences against children, whether physical or emotional. It is one of the most terrible of the many sins into which people may fall. In the vivid and extreme language which he sometimes used in his teaching, Jesus tells the

Twelve that even bodily mutilation is better than spiritual condemnation. We are all to cast out evil, not by literal following of these frightening words but by turning away from the temptations which beset us, by shunning apparent pleasures which are leading us into sin. There is evil enough in the world, and those who love the Lord should not blame other people for it but look to their own failings. The last verse of this reading speaks of angels in the eternal presence of God, charged with particular care of his little ones in this world. It is both a beautiful and a challenging thought for this day. The heavenly beings we call angels sometimes come into our world as messengers and protectors. They remind us that there are more things in God's creation than we can know with our mortal senses. St Michael stands as the representative of wonderful works of God beyond our understanding.

Glory to thee, Almighty God, for the holy angels who serve thee in heaven and guard us on earth. Restore in me the innocence of childhood, guide me to protect the weak and vulnerable, especially the little children, and to walk before thee in true humility of spirit.

'Twas on a Holy Thursday, their innocent faces clean,
The children walking two and two, in red and blue and green,
Grey-headed beadles walk'd before, with wands as white as
    snow,
Till into the high dome of Paul's they like Thames waters flow.

O what a multitude they seem'd, these flowers of London town!
Seated in companies, they sit with radiance all their own.
The hum of multitudes was there, but multitudes of lambs,
Thousands of little boys and girls raising their innocent hands.

Now like a mighty wind they raise to Heaven the voice of song,
Or like harmonious thunderings the seats of Heaven among.
Beneath them sit the aged men, wise guardians of the poor;
Then cherish pity, lest you drive an angel from your door.

William Blake (1756–1827) 'Holy Thursday', *Songs of Innocence*

St Luke the Evangelist
Luke 10.1–7

The third Gospel and the Acts of the Apostles are accepted as the work of Luke. His Gospel is particularly striking for parables which do not appear elsewhere, and for its tone of tenderness and compassion. He gives us the fullest Nativity story, the main source for our Christmas devotions. He alone gives us the great parables known as the Prodigal Son and the Good Samaritan. In the Acts he gives a precious record of the first years of the Church. He was a companion of Paul, who affectionately calls him 'the beloved physician' (Colossians 4.14), and was with him even to the last days in Rome. He seems to have been a Gentile, one of the earliest converts. There is probably no truth in the legend that he was an artist, but the idea does accord with the skill with which he describes people and events. The Gospel for his day reminds us yet again that there were many more than the Twelve who followed Jesus in his years of ministry. Seventy are sent out to preach the good news. They are like precursors of the apostles; the great story is not yet complete, but there is ground to be prepared. In human terms, they are not given much encouragement, being likened to sheep put out into the company of the dreaded wolves. Their trust is in the Good Shepherd whose love watches over them in danger and hardship. They are to forsake all worldly comforts and, like their Master, depend on hospitality wherever they can find it. They are the first of those who will give up all for Jesus: the missionaries, the religious, the travelling evangelists of centuries to come. Women and men whose secular careers seemed full of promise have given up everything for the service of their Lord. The labourers have always been few, but they have been faithful and zealous, offering back to God the gifts that he had given them. Their faith gives comfort also to all who have accepted the cost of following in faith, even in little things as well as great. The labourers still are few, especially in parts of the world which greatly need assurance and hope. We should continue to pray for vocations, a need which is too often overlooked by a Church beset with its domestic problems. All Christians have a vocation to be faithful in their working and domestic lives, no less precious to God. Not many are called to the special work of God's harvesting: but many are called to give up a little for the sake of the greater. There is no human ability that cannot be used in the divine purpose. Praise be to God for Luke, for his Gospel and for his example. The reading for today has a message which is typical of his work: peace, received and given.

Most loving God, the great Healer of sickness in body and in soul, thou art ever near to those who serve without regard to self. Give me that same spirit of service, show me thy purpose for me in this life, keep me faithful in the journey to life eternal.

It has been said that there are on the battlefield, defeats as glorious as victories. That is true also of the daily defeats of the soul in the struggle which we begin afresh every day, making new plans to do better and experimenting with new ideas and methods in order to succeed. That is what the Gospel declares: 'Happy is the servant whom when his Master cometh He shall find . . .' Find how? Victorious? Triumphant? His task fully accomplished? No! Rather he who shall be found watching, vigilant, wide awake; that is to say looking after the things which are not going well and putting them right, time after time, That is our really great merit in the sight of God.

Henri de Tourville (1842–1903) *Letters of Direction*

St Simon and St Jude
John 15.17–27

We know little about these two men, who are briefly mentioned in the Gospels and have been linked for celebration on this day for many centuries. Simon is described as 'the Zealot', a member of the movement most strongly resistant to Roman rule. Jude is accepted as the author of the short and admonitory Epistle which bears his name and gives severe warnings about threats to the new Church.

At the Last Supper he asks Jesus whether the divine revelation is for the few or will be given to the whole world (John 14.22). The reply is that God will receive all who love him and show their love by obedience to his word. The Gospel for their day takes us back to the great words of teaching on the eve of the Passion, words both of encouragement and of warning. To be chosen to carry on the work of Jesus in this world is both privilege and danger. Many people have hated him, and will hate them, because he has confronted them with the reality of their sinful state, giving no flattery but preaching the need for repentance. Still today, perhaps more than ever, there is resentment of anything which seems to challenge an individual's way of life. The Twelve are reminded yet again of their position of service: they cannot expect to escape the opposition aroused by the Lord himself. But they will not be left to fight alone. The Holy Sprit will guide and strengthen them for whatever lies before them. The privilege of being in the service of God is far greater than any social rank or influence. All are made one in Christ and no human honour can compare with being called to his service. We have no power that does not come from him. To follow where he leads is to take on, in whatever slight degree, the possibility of a share in his suffering and in his ministry. When Christians start getting proud of their achievements, when they think that they can do great things in their own strength, when they would like the privileges of faith without its responsibilities, they may do well to remember the words of Jesus, 'The servant is not greater than the Lord.'

Thanks be to thee, O God, for the words of truth which have guided thy people from age to age. May I stand firm in the strength of the Holy Spirit, to know the privilege of service, and to obey thy great commandment of love.

Among our Lord's twelve Apostles there were two of the same name of Judas, both chosen to be, as it were, Angels of light; one continuing to be really such, and the other ending most miserably; both, as it were, calling out to us to remind us of our danger; the one by his warning words, the other by his sad example. St Jude's Epistle is altogether of admonition, and stern, mournful prophecy of evil; but these evils he urges as incentives to us of more earnest care and diligence, beginning and ending with words of encouragement, if we thus live. 'But, ye beloved, building up yourselves on your most holy faith, praying in the Holy Ghost, keep yourselves in the love of God.' This is, as it were, his one lesson of advice for this day.

Isaac Williams (1802–1865) *Sermons* 1855

All Saints' Day
Matthew 5.1–12

At the end of the Sanctorale, the yearly cycle of commemorating the saints, we praise God for all those, known or unknown to history, whose lives have been marked by singular holiness. There are many who might be called the 'official saints', named in the New Testament or canonized by one or more of the Churches. There are far more who have passed through this world, given their witness, and been forgotten within a generation. They were not all 'nice' people in the comfortable sense that we like to expect of each other. Many were eccentric, difficult to live with, even neurotic: but they were marked by a deep awareness of the God in whom they trusted and the desire to live close to his holiness in this world as they aspired towards eternity. But we are all 'called to be saints', the words written by Paul to the new Christians at Corinth whom he would severely censure for their moral and doctrinal faults (1 Corinthians 1.2). The Greek word he uses is *hagioi* 'holy ones', an attribute of God himself as in the thrice-repeated 'Holy, Holy, Holy' (Revelation 4.8). It is with this wonderful and awesome challenge that we read the Gospel for today, the beginning of the Sermon on the Mount. Jesus speaks to his disciples of the blessings which God bestows on many as they live their ordinary lives in this world. Some are uplifting, like the call to be meek and peacemakers; others are contrary to human expectations, like the privilege of suffering for faith. To accept our own holiness as Christians is as difficult as truly to accept the depth of our sinfulness. Perhaps it is more difficult: we are too well aware of our sins but, unless we are culpably complacent, we seldom find in ourselves anything resembling sainthood. But it is there, not by our own merits and strivings, but because we are granted a share in the righteousness of Jesus, our sins forgiven, the image of God restored in us. We may try humbly and with prayer to acknowledge the grace we have received and live more worthily of our call to be saints. And we may recognize and honour the saintliness of those who have a grace different from that which we might expect from a casual knowledge of them.

It is not influence, power, or even great virtue that is the mark of sainthood. The grace of God which changes and sanctifies ordinary people is the glory of his kingdom. The note of this day is praise and thanksgiving. At the same time, there is a solemn reminder that the ways of God are not our ways. He takes our false values and transforms them into holiness.

Almighty God, with whom thy saints in heaven rejoice, and by whom thy people on earth are guided, we praise thee for the holy fellowship of all who come to thee in faith. Keep me mindful of my calling, deliver me from all that is unworthy of it, and strengthen me in the holiness which is thy gift and thy will.

We crowd these all up into one day; we mingle together in the brief remembrance of an hour all the choicest deeds, the holiest lives, the noblest labours, the most precious sufferings, which the sun ever saw. Even the least of those Saints were the contemplation of many days – even the names of them, if read in our Service, would outrun many settings and risings of the light – even one passage in the life of one of them were more than sufficient for a long discourse. Martyrs and Confessors, Rulers and Doctors of the Church, devoted Ministers and Religious brethren, kings of the earth and all people, princes and judges of the earth, young men and maidens, old men and children, the first fruits of all ranks, ages, and callings, gathered each in his own time into the paradise of God.

J. H. Newman (1801–1890) *Parochial and Plain Sermons*

Index of Names and Sources